MILESSTYLE

The Fashion of Miles Davis

Michael Stradford

Cover photograph: Courtesy of Anthony Barbosa

Pg. 130: Photograph of Miles Davis by Jeff Sedlik © 1989

Vincent Wilburn Jr. photo courtesy of Corey Nickols

Cover Design: Michael Stradford

ISBN: 978-164786557-3

FIRST EDITION

MILESSTYLE

FOR SYBIL AND DON

CONTENTS

ACKNOWLEDGMENTS

My sincere gratitude and appreciation to all those who lent their time and assistance to help make this project possible:

Andrea Aranow, Anthony Barboza, Mathieu Bitton, Lloyd Boston, Dr. Todd Boyd, Robert Baruc, Ron Carter, Betty Davis, Frances Davis, Charlie Davidson, Mikel Elam, Bryan Ferry, Isaac Ferry, Kim Gagne, Michael Henderson, Reggie Hudlin, Darryl Jones, Quincy Jones, Dr. Donald Kilhefner, Lenny Kravitz, Susan Lennon, Jason Medley, Marcus Miller, Monica L. Miller, Issey Miyake, Faulu Mtume, James Mtume, Gersha Phillips, Darryl Porter, Jeff Sedlik, Michael Shulman, Wendy Smith-Baruc, Vincent Wilburn, Jr., Emilian White

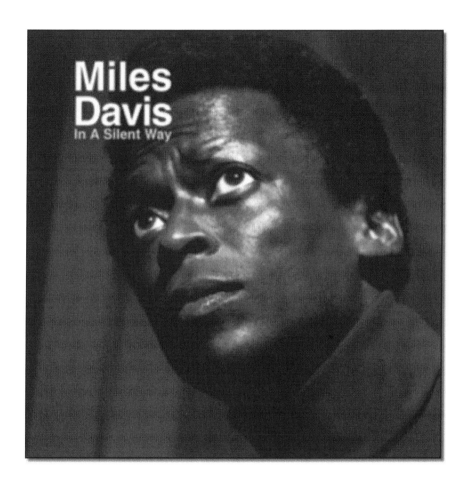

INTRODUCTION

'It knocks me out to be me. It really kills me'.

-Miles Davis

I saw Miles Davis before I ever heard a note of his music. It was in my father's 1969 Cadillac Coupe de Ville. During the week, my Pops used his Chevrolet station wagon to load and unload supplies for his delicatessen. But every Sunday, he'd roll up the garage door and park the Caddy in the driveway and lovingly spend a few hours making the car look showroom new.

Later in the evening, my father would load me and my mother into the cleanest car in Cleveland, then we'd go for dinner and a drive. I'd sit in the spacious white leather back seat, going through his case of 8-track tapes. The Temptations, Lou Rawls, Aretha Franklin were among the warm and familiar faces that would greet me. On this particular Sunday, I saw a new face. A dark-skinned man with a furrowed brow, staring intently at who knows what. This was my initial introduction to Miles Davis.

The 8-track album was *In A Silent Way*. I wish I could say that it was instant love, but it wasn't. While I didn't know what I was expecting, it certainly wasn't the strange, avant-garde sounds that came through the car speakers. I didn't like it, nor did my parents. My dad didn't know how the 8-track got in his case and it was quickly removed, to be replaced by Aretha Franklin doing her thing live at the Filmore.

After that introduction, every once in a while, I'd come across a photo of Miles Davis, never smiling, always looking either deep in concentration or very pissed off. Every now and then I'd hear his name attached to words like 'militant', 'rude' 'rebellious' and 'evil'. He was often referred to as 'The Prince of Darkness' and from what I could see, the name wasn't so farfetched. I kept my distance from the Dark Prince, preferring the comfort of the Jackson Five and Al Green. Miles Davis was off my radar for years, until he wasn't. I don't exactly remember the details of what brought me back to him; I remember friends like Roy Emory trying so hard to get me interested in jazz, but I was having none of that. However, in the early stage of my radio career at WCIN in Cincinnati in 1981, everyone was abuzz with Miles Davis' return after he'd gone underground for five years. I didn't really notice his absence since he wasn't an artist that I kept track of. At this point I was a devotee' of 80s hitmakers Hall & Oates, Prince and a new guy named Luther Vandross.

In 1981, Miles had released his first album of new music in several years, *The Man with the Horn*, and came to Cincinnati for a concert to promote both the album and his return to the stage. I decided to go to the show because a part of me thought while I had no interest or appreciation for the man or his music, perhaps years later I could go fond of it and I would be glad that attended the concert.

It was one of the strangest concerts I'd ever been to. Miles came out in a baggy pink jumpsuit, wearing a white knit cap with the word 'Pepe' stitched across the front and a pair of clogs. He looked frail and roamed back and forth across the stage like an old man who was in dire need of relief. He'd blurt out a few notes on the horn once in a while and directed his much younger band through a series of aggressively loud, almost rock riffs that barely flirted with a melody. Miles never said a word to the audience, but as he shuffled off at the end of the evening, he stopped quite abruptly in his tracks, looked out at the adoring crowd and waved his hand, sending the place into a frenzy, and then he was gone, leaving me scratching my head.

A few nights later, while programming the music for my overnight jazz show on WCIN (1480 AM), I stumbled across an album cover featuring a dapper, chilled Miles Davis holding his horn, wearing a dark suit with a polka dot tie, with a look on his face that seemed to be between two moments. The album, *My Funny Valentine: Miles Davis in Concert*, got my attention.

3

'My Funny Valentine', a 1937 show tune written for the stage musical 'Babes in Arms' by Richard Rogers and Lorenz Hart, is a perfect song. It's virtually indestructible, having survived all manner of interpretation by the widest range of artists imaginable, more than 600 and counting. Based on my limited experience with Miles, I thought he'd be the first artist to dismember this gem, but I was curious. Something about his look suggested that I should take a chance on him again. When I took the album out of the jacket and saw that 'My Funny Valentine' had a runtime of over fifteen minutes, I just knew I was about to be bombarded with more indecipherable Martian audio sounds. But I forged on.

When the needle touched the vinyl, everything changed. First, the music was acoustic, not a single electronic instrument was heard anywhere. Secondly, the band had a unified sound, warm and gentle. But what was most striking to me was the tone that came out of Miles Davis' trumpet. Fragile, haunted and pensive, Davis displayed a vulnerability that I wasn't ready for. When I got off the air, I listened to the rest of the album on repeat, finding it hard to believe that this was the same screaming banshee who had just left Cincinnati only days before.

From that point on, I began to familiarize myself with Miles Davis' vast catalog of music. I found in short order that the period from 1950-66 was the sweet spot for me. *Bitches Brew*, *On the Corner* and the bulk of his electric music wouldn't reach me until the new millennium. I enjoyed his controversial Warner Bros. albums almost immediately and still have much love for his take on 'Human Nature' and 'Time After Time', even though jazz purists tend to turn their noses up at it with the argument that a master was supposedly wasting time with 'slight pop music puffery'.

As a man who's changed the face of music more than once, there is no shortage of words written about Miles Davis. I began to read, articles, reviews and interviews, curious to find out how such a volatile, controversial figure could come up with some of the most sensitive, heartbreaking music that I'd ever listened to.

Of course, no book could provide the perfect answer, but they offered clues. Born a Gemini, that helped explain the almost split personality of the elegant sophisticate and the crude, rude rebel. Growing up short and dark-skinned Davis probably had to develop a thick skin pretty quickly and the ability to look out for himself. He grew up in a family that was quite wealthy, and his father instilled in him a belief in his own ability, drilling into his head to never accept less than he was worth from anyone, black or white.

I also read about how hard he studied. The long practice hours he had to endure, and I also read about his ability to find and groom great musicians. There were great stories about him and fast cars and beautiful women, getting beat up by the police, boxing with Sugar Ray Robinson, becoming a junkie and kicking the habit cold turkey. Countless examples of Davis his mind, cursing out anyone who he thought deserved it, fly clothes and the legendary brownstone on the upper west side of New York are among the consistent tales told about the temperamental trumpeter.

It became impossible for me to separate the artist from the art. It seemed the word 'Cool' was coined specifically so that there is a word good enough to describe Miles Davis. The way he prowled the stage like a panther during the golden age, was cool. It wasn't rehearsed or choreographed; you could feel the honesty in it and instantly understand that this was who he was. The concise, economical movements, the neatly cropped hair and perfectly tailored suits were brand management before the word crept into our lexicon. He was just doing what came naturally in a way that no one had ever done before. Although to say that he was unaware of the impact of his attitude and physical presentation would be a short-sighted and lazy assessment of his canny marketing sensibility.

Over the years, I have collected a number of books on Miles Davis. At the time of this writing, Amazon (US) lists more than two dozen available books on Miles Davis, along with several more that are out of print. Everything from examining specific albums, to bios, a volume on his paintings and even books that put a microscope on his individual trumpet solos, can be yours with a few clicks of your mouse. Like most things, some are good, a couple of them are great, and a few of them are quite off point, missing the mark. But whether weak or strong, every book on Miles Davis that I've read has always offered at least one thing that I didn't know before reading it.

So why am I writing another treatise on Miles Davis? Miles Davis was a restless, ever-changing creator. Whether it was through music, cooking or painting, he spoke with a voice that was inimitably his own. The bulk of the existing Miles Davis library puts an appropriate spotlight on his music. For example, a recently released book examines his painting and pencil work. *MilesStyle* concentrates on an often mentioned but rarely focused area of Davis' life: his love for clothes and his unique sense of fashion.

Miles' sartorial splendor wasn't lost on those in the know. *Esquire* magazine named him one of the 75 best-dressed men of all time, while *GQ* accorded him the title of best-dressed musician <u>ever</u>. I don't think there are many men who could be beaten bloody by the police and still manage to look cool. That was Miles Davis.

There are many iconic photos of Miles, most feature a grim, intense or distracted looking man, slight in stature but large in intensity. If one looks past the look on his face, the viewer is often greeted by a beautifully composed photograph, with the subject immaculately dressed in a dark suit, sometimes a khaki jacket and occasionally a fine tuxedo, tailored perfectly to accentuate his features.

In the forties, Miles Davis wore the baggy, oversized suits of the day until Dexter Gordon shamed him for dressing 'country'. It would be a few years before he discovered his own personal style, peaking in the mid-fifties through the early seventies, then flying off the rails during the last (visually assaultive) decade of his life. But he was never dull.

MilesStyle was originally intended to be a coffee table book, as a visual representation of his personal style would have been the best way to introduce the world to his flair. Unfortunately, the cost to license images made that untenable, and while several publishers liked the content and concept, none was willing to stake their money to help bring it to life.

However, I felt like the information I was able to find and the interviews that accompany the biographical material offers some fresh, unique insights into both the Miles Davis mystique and Miles Davis the real human being. Perhaps somewhere down the road there will arise an opportunity to revisit this book with more illustrations than this first edition.

Each chapter begins with a brief overview of where Miles Davis was at during the period covered. The assumption is that if you're a fan of Miles Davis, you probably have at least a decent working knowledge of his history. And if you're new to Miles, hopefully the content in *MilesStyle* will inspire you to read more and find more books that cover his music, life and career in more detail than is provided here.

In addition to the research, the most exciting and satisfying part of this project for me was the interview process. Throughout the book you'll read exclusive conversations with people who knew him well, personally and professionally, as well as tastemakers who provide a unique social context for the man and his wardrobe. Everyone I spoke with had at least one great Miles Davis story to share, usually more than one.

When I started this project, the focus was largely on Miles Davis's closet, throughout the years he lived and performed. As I began interviewing people that knew him and even those who only knew of him, I realized that *MilesStyle* was more than just conversations about clothes. Everyone that I spoke with had a story about Miles that was illuminating, whether it was about music, clothes or how to cook a gourmet meal. Within each story was a peek into the overall style of the man. He had a particular way that he walked in the world, one that bled into everything that he touched.

As you read some of the interviews, while you'll notice that most of them concentrate on his fashion sense, you'll equally find out that they all provided a sense of his unique take on the world. I left those interviews in their authentic state without editing them because they effectively illustrate Miles' style in all things, regardless of the subject. These conversations provide the reader with a richer 'gumbo' to digest, if you will.

Miles Davis has been called many things, including 'the Picasso of Jazz'. As a man who kept evolving and banging at the ceiling, the comparison to the brilliant but prickly painter made sense. But when it comes to his sense of personal style, aside from perhaps Lenny Kravitz, there's never been anyone to compare him to that didn't feel like it was an unfit comparison.

When *Esquire* magazine listed their picks for the 50 most stylish musicians of the last 50 years, there would be a photo with an explanation of what made each musician so stylish. When it got to Miles Davis, the description simply read, 'Miles Davis'. Nothing else needed to be said.

1. BIRTH OF THE COOL: 1926-1949

'I have thought that prejudice and curiosity have been responsible for what I have done in music'.

-Miles Davis

Miles Dewey Davis blew his first solo when the doctor popped him on the butt on the 25th of May 1926. Miles was born in Alton, Illinois, about 15 miles north of St. Louis, considered part of the Greater St. Louis metropolitan area.

The proud parents were Miles Sr., a very successful oral surgeon and dentist, who was also a gentleman pig farmer, and Cleota, an accomplished violinist. As Dr. Davis' practice continued to grow, he moved the family, including their daughter Dorothy, who was a year older than Miles, to East St. Louis, Illinois, across from Mississippi river, minutes from the more cosmopolitan St. Louis. In 1928, Miles' younger brother Vernon was born.

In short order, in a bold move, Dr. Davis again moved the family, this time to an all-white neighborhood in East St. Louis. Dr. Davis, who went on to earn three degrees, was a successful and highly competent black man, who liked nice cars, fine clothes and refused to be limited by demands of the white majority of the day. This was a lesson that he passed on to his son, who embraced his father's philosophy.

As an adult, Miles was known for his lack of tolerance for prejudice, never hesitating to speak his mind about it. In his *Playboy* interview with Alex Haley, Miles said, "very few white people really know what Negroes really feel like. A lot of white people have never even been in the company of an intelligent Negro. But you can hardly meet a white person, especially a white man, that don't think he's qualified to tell you all about Negroes."

But fortunately, Miles didn't spend his entire childhood dealing with prejudice. His mother was a music aficionado who exposed him to classical music, as well as cherished 78rpm discs by Duke Ellington and Art Tatum.

When Miles would venture to 'the country' in rural Arkansas to visit his grandfather, he would be immersed in the popular gospel and country music that was the trend at the time. Back in East St. Louis, late-night radio introduced him to the swinging big bands that captured his imagination and wouldn't let go.

While they were often at odds, Miles' mother gets credit from her son for two of his most notable attributes. "She was a very glamorous woman who was into all kinds of hats and things. She was always dressed to kill. I got my looks from my mother and also my love of clothes and sense of style. I guess you could say I got whatever artistic talent I have from her also" *(autobiography, pg.*14*)*.

Mrs. Davis may have been the first, but she wasn't the only one to make a stylistic impression on young Miles. "My favorite dresser was Fred Astaire, when I was in school. Cary Grant could dress alright, but I liked Fred Astaire. He was my size. I'd get them collars (like he wore) for five cents and them shirts for ten, but you couldn't turn your neck!" *(Miles Davis Radio Project part one)*.

Miles' mother was also looking to build on her son's interest in music by steering him towards a focus on classical, intending to buy him a violin as a first instrument, but Dr. Davis beat her to the punch, gifting his son with his first trumpet when he was about ten years old.

Miles took the trumpet seriously, shifting his interest in boxing and other sports to a single-minded approach in understanding and mastering his instrument. Schooled by Elwood Buchanan, music teacher at Lincoln High School, Miles famously learned early on not to rely on a vibrato sound but to develop a tone that was strong, clear and distinctive.

The practice and commitment paid off when he met local trumpeter Clark Terry, who initially blew him off when the young musician interrupted Terry's designs on a young lady that he was trying to get to know.

In addition to being a ladies' man, Clark Terry was handsome, had great personal style as well as a unique playing style. He was commonly regarded as a superior player and was well regarded for his hip but friendly personality. Miles recalls, "Clark had on this hip coat and this bad, beautiful scarf around his neck. He was wearing butcher boy shoes and a bad hat cocked ace-deuce. I told him I could also tell he was a trumpet player by the hip shit he was wearing" *(autobiography, pg. 33)*. It's not hard to see why

Terry made such a profound influence on young Miles Davis.

Being schooled by Buchanan and Terry, Miles quickly became a part of the St. Louis music scene, playing wherever he could, whenever he could, keeping late hours but still getting to school on time. His rapid development led to Davis being invited to join Eddie Randle's Rhumboogie Orchestra at a time he was still relatively inexperienced. Randle, himself a trumpeter, helped Miles develop his chops and theories about music. Miles dedication and ability to catch on quickly earned him his place as the musical director of the band.

Even though he was a young player, fashion was already important to young Davis. "I was making about $85 a week playing in Eddie Randle's band and with other people, and I was buying myself some hip Brooks Brothers suits' (*autobiography, pg. 47*).

The Rhumboogie Orchestra also opened wide the world of possibility for Miles by exposing him to some of the biggest names in jazz on the national scene. Realizing that it wasn't just that he played with them, but that they equally respected his talent, helped the young horn player build even more confidence in his ability and taste.

While Miles worked on his chops, he was also considering his other options, going to dental school or joining the navy. But his future was never really in question. As he assessed the potential of his future endeavors, jazz was also finding its own way, led by musicians like Dizzy Gillespie, who helped hip him to harmonic theory, Charlie 'Yardbird' Parker and vocalist Billy Eckstine, who ran one of the most respected outfits in all of jazz. In 1944, when Eckstine stopped in St. Louis and heard Miles, he snapped him up. That gig only lasted two weeks, but its effect was a lasting one. In short order, Miles moved to the center of the jazz world: New York City.

Leaving Irene, the young mother of Cheryl, his first child (of which there would be three), Miles was accepted into Julliard and set out to find Bird and Dizzy, with plans to pick up where they left off when they all played with the Eckstine band. It was more than a notion to find Bird, but when eventually did, they played together regularly.

Julliard provided Miles with a sound basis in music theory, but he was quickly soured by the stiff, formal approach to music, based on European and classical compositions, which was the sole foundation of music at Julliard. This resistance was further fueled by his nightly excursions into the more liberal and exciting world of jazz that awaited him every night in New York, as he sat in regularly at clubs like Minton's Playhouse and a variety of 52nd street venues.

Aware that he was a country mouse in the big city, in addition to having a baby face, Miles went to great lengths to project an air of maturity and sophistication. Photos from the era show him with 'processed' hair and a barely visible mustache. He's generally seen in suits that, while trendy for the time, virtually swallow his slight frame with their extra thick shoulder pants and parachute full trousers.

Miles' look was a reminder that World War II was nearing its conclusion. During the war, clothes were much more subtle and practical. The extra fabric that had been used for double-breasted jackets, men's pant cuffs and vests, were now styled in new ways that minimized waste and flamboyance, showing the proper respect for the severity of war.

Once the war was over, great natural fabrics, bold styles and elegant accessories came back and more often than not, jazz musicians were leading the way, expressing themselves as creatively through clothes as they had through music.

Miles would come to be known as one of the best-dressed men of the twentieth century, but in the mid-forties, he needed some help with his fashion sense. When Miles first arrived in New York, he remembered making enough money to buy his long-admired Brooks Brothers suits. But his perspective on fashion would soon be expanded by Coleman 'Bean' Hawkins, Charlie Rice and Dexter Gordon.

Saxophonist Hawkins or 'Bean' as he was known was very well regarded by Miles, who states very plainly his affection for the easy to get along with composer in his autobiography. That feeling was mutual, as Hawkins would often give Miles clothes that he bought from a fashionable shop in midtown Manhattan.

Drummer Charlie Rice blew Miles' mind with the revelation of custom-made clothing, which had a lifelong impression on the young trumpeter. As Miles recounts, "Charlie used to make his own suits and he made some for Bean. Man, them suits was motherfuckers. I said to him, 'Goddamn Charlie, why don't you make me one of them suits?' He said for me to just get the material and he would, free of charge. So, I did. And he made me a bad double-breasted suit that I used to wear to death. I think a lot of them pictures that they took of me around 1945 to 1947 I was wearing Charlie Rice's suits. After that, I have always got my suits made when I had the money" (*autobiography pg. 78*).

But the toughest lesson to learn about fashion in the big city, and clearly the most entertaining is the one taught to Miles by the elegant saxophonist Dexter Gordon. Miles admired the way clothes fell on the tall, slender Gordon. It wasn't uncommon to see Gordon sauntering around New York in finely tailored double-breasted suits with deep pleats and two-inch cuffs.

Even though he thought Gordon was as sharp as a tack, Miles still thought his Brooks Brothers look was the business, until Dexter set him straight. "Jim, you can't hang with us looking and dressing like that. Why don't you wear some other shit, Jim? You gotta get some vines" (*autobiography, pg. 111*). Gordon suggested Miles visit a clothing store in Midtown called F&M, in order to update his look.

Miles protested and instead, attempted to bring Dexter over to his way of thinking, trying to get him to appreciate the Brooks Brothers style. But Gordon was having none of it. As Miles remembered, Dexter told him "Miles, that ain't it, cause the shit ain't hip. See, it ain't got nothin' to do with money; it's got something to do with hipness, Jim ('Jim' was common slang for jazz musicians to call each other, similar to the use of 'man' or 'bro' today), and that shit you got on ain't nowhere near hip. You gotta get some of them big-shouldered suits and Mr. B shirts if you want to be hip, Miles'. Gordon wanted to be sure he got through to Miles, so he continued preaching the men's fashion gospel. 'I can't be seen with nobody wearing no square shit like you be wearing. And you playing in Bird's band? The hippest band in the world? Man, you oughta know better" (*autobiography, pg. 111*).

Gordon's words cut deep. Miles was hurt because of his deep admiration for Gordon as a man and a musician. But he didn't let his pride hold him back. The end result was an ill-fitting gray suit that swallowed the diminutive Miles whole. The suit can be seen in several early photos of Miles from his publicity shots from 1948, along with a short lived pencil thin mustache and a 'process' hairstyle, also called a 'conk', a technique of straightening tightly curled or naturally kinky hair with a hot comb of metal and congolene, a hair straightener created out of lye. When Gordon saw the new look, Miles recalled, "Dexter came up to me ginning that big grin of his and towering over me, patting me on my back, saying, 'Yea, Jim, now you looking like something, now you hip. You can hang with us'" (*autobiography, pg. 111*).

In 1945, Miles joined Charlie Parker's quintet after Dizzy Gillespie left. The next year, he made his first recording as a leader with the Miles Davis Sextet, but continued off and on as a member of Parker's band, recording some memorable sides until Parker's erratic behavior coupled with his inability or total refusal to pay his players resulted in Miles leaving for good in 1948.

As they say, 'when one door closes, another one opens'. That that was the case as Miles developed what would be one of the most important relationships of his life, both musically and professionally, when he met arranger Gil Evans. The thoughtful and creative Evans found a simpatico voice in Miles and their partnership would evolve into a great friendship that lasted throughout their lives.

Their first historic collaboration resulted in the creation of a nonet, based on an idea to create a band whose instrumentation would mirror the human voice. The group was a mixed-race, nine-piece, horn-driven band led by Miles. The nonet made several recordings in late 1949 through early 1950. The band featured John Lewis on piano, Al McKibbon on bass, Max Roach on drums, Gerry Mulligan played baritone sax, Junior Collins on French horn, Bill Barber on tuba, Lee Konitz on alto sax, and of course, Miles on trumpet. The result was the legendary 'Birth of the Cool' album, which wouldn't be released until 1956.

The album was initially stillborn commercially when it was first unveiled to the public, but musicians who were also exploring similar musical ideas at the same time, adopted it as one of their own. West Coast musicians like

Stan Getz, Woody Herman and Chet Baker were some of the better-known faces of the sub-genre' of 'cool jazz', music with easy tempos, subdued melodies and smooth or light execution, and these faces, all white, brought Miles no small amount of resentment.

Cool jazz, Bird's undependability and Julliard's rigid program caused some bumpy roads for the East St. Louis transplant. But for the most part, Miles' initial venture to New York was a great adventure; one that he embraced with a creative enthusiasm that would see him through the trials of the upcoming decade and result in some of the most memorable music of the 20th century.

Birth of the Cool
CONVOS

Clark Terry *was one of Jazz music's true giants. A trumpet player of the highest order who taught Miles Davis, Quincy Jones, Herbie Hancock, Wynton Marsalis and*

many more, Clark or 'Mumbles' as he was popularly called, was known for his unique vocal scatting style, was an educator, a bandleader and a member of the Tonight Show Band, among his other accomplishments. 'Keep On, Keepin On', released in 2014, is a moving documentary about the relationship between Terry and one of his final students. It captures a physically debilitated man whose insight, humor and generosity illustrates the magnitude of his humanity.

Following my interview with Quincy Jones, 'Q' connected me with Clark for a brief chat about Miles. While he was battling diabetes and a number of other ailments, Clark was eager to talk about Miles, and fashion in the forties. Clark's kind and gracious wife, Gwen, was there to gently prod his memory and clarify some parts of our chat, but Clark was ready to go. 93 years young when we spoke, Clark Terry transitioned on February 21, 2015.

What did clothes mean to a black man in the forties and fifties, particularly guys like you, who were concentrating on expanding an art form?

Well, the first thing I should tell you is that I come from a big family, seven girls and three boys. I always got the hand me downs, and sometimes I had to wear my sisters' things! I used to go to the second-hand store near my house and buy pants and shoes. I was pretty interested in dressing nice. I went to thrift shops, hand me down stores, to me they were brand new.

Whenever I see photos of jazz players, everybody was sharp.

That was the thing in those days. We'd all try to outdo each other dressing. You had to look sharp to be sharp. I just had a desire to look better than most people. My first nice suit was a blue double-breasted pin striped suit that I took my first promo photos in. I always love a double-breasted suit. In those days, I was a little cat and a double-breasted made me feel bigger (laughs).

I lived in St. Louis in the mid-eighties. Fashion wasn't a high priority when I was there. Was it a stylish city during your time there?

In our circle it was, for those who could afford it. But not everybody could afford it.

When you first met Miles, did you have to school him on how to dress?

I was pretty much in the limelight then, so he used me as kind of a model, but he would come up with all kinds of ideas on his own. He was the first person that I saw wear a suit with a raglan sleeve.

What did you think of his personal style?

Well, it didn't bother me too much, because I was busy working on my own thing (laughs). He could afford better clothes, because his dad was a doctor.

It sounds like you were great friends.

I loved him very much. He was a very nice kid before he got mangled up with that stuff (drugs). I befriended him and he took advantage of me, and he swiped things from me, but he didn't mean any harm. He was a little guy and I was a little bigger. We'd be in a bar and he order some drinks and put his change on the bar. I'd take his change and put it in my pocket, 'cause I was a pretty good boxer in those days.

(At this point, Gwen recounted some memories that Clark shared with her that she relayed to me.)

Not only was he a sharp dresser, all the cats had custom shoes and beautiful socks, they had gorgeous accessories like jewelry and hats. They got manicures and pedicures, they had massages, and they were very particular about their bodies because they worked out. It was more than the clothes they wore; it was a state of mind. Their valets had to be dressed up, the women they were with had to be dressed up too. Clark bought me a whole new wardrobe when we got married. I didn't have the kind of clothes that would accent his style. He had all kinds of hats handkerchiefs, suits, custom-made everything! Looking good and smelling good was the status.

Clark had so many different types of shoes. When he'd go on cruises, he'd wear sandals that curled up at the toe with a bell at the tip! (Clark interjects: 'here he comes, cause the bells would ringing!') (laughs)

Clark had strict dress requirements for his students, his big bands, what have you. They couldn't come up on the stage in baggy jeans and all of that. No. They all had to have suits.

Clark, if you could describe Miles in one word, what would it be?

Just one word? (long pause). 'Interesting', I think interesting (laughs).

Lloyd Boston has been working in fashion and television for twenty years. A former VP of Art Direction for Tommy Hilfiger, Lloyd is an accomplished author of four books, focusing on style for both men and women, with topics ranging from history to

'how-to', with his first book, 'Men of Color', offering a historical examination of the impact of the African-American male as it pertains to personal style and self-expression. Among his television roles as both host and style contributor are stints on the Style Network, HGTV, Fine Living, E! Entertainment and the Today Show.

Why do you think fashion and style mean so much to people of color, particularly men?

Well, we have a long history of understanding and valuing image as it relates to us socially. As kind of marginalized people of color dating back hundreds of years, I think we were quick to understand that our image was one of the few things that we fully owned and were able to control. So when it comes time to present ourselves in public in hopes of finding equality whether it's on the job front or just in social interaction, we know that this is the place we can control the way people see us, before we even have a chance to speak.

For men, Black, White or otherwise, it became even more important to Black men, who had to keep a roof over their family's head, raise their children, provide for their family and community. Our clothing and accessories showed the world how serious we were about wanting to fit in, to succeed and thrive. As we began to make strides toward economic equality, we started to understand that this was a big skill set for us, as it not only helped us by day, but at night when it was time to express ourselves. Much of it relates back to our African ancestry, you name the tribe, we have always been a very expressive culture and I think that hasn't changed to this day.

That's a great opening statement to set the context for this conversation. Now we segue to the man of the hour. When <u>you</u> think of Miles Davis, what is the first thing that comes to mind?

Someone who was not only a trendsetter, but also kind of a rainmaker. Very similar to other style icons who are often times in the fringe of style but lead the changes in mainstream style. I would put him in the category of Grace Jones, or someone as modern as Lady Gaga. Or someone earlier than him, like Cab Calloway: big, over the top expressive style that isn't always adapted by the mainstream right away, but you find that will trickle into mainstream culture after that person has moved on from that particular style. He was never fearful to select and express himself with style that wasn't 'approved' to be acceptable. When I think of his different looks through the decades, he was always reinventing himself through style, but it was never anything he wanted credit for, it was always his love of clothing, artifice and accessories, that was not unlike other men of color that you see in jazz clubs, nightclubs or even the church.

In the fifties and early to mid-sixties, Miles dressed in a relatively simple way: sleek, well-cut suits and casual wear. When we look at the last ten to fifteen years of his life, his style got more flamboyant with the genie pants, big-shouldered jackets and hair weave that gave way to wigs. What do you think of his stylistic evolution?

Early on, he did sport a very casual, chic, continental look that the American man in the 50s found appealing. It was inspired by certain European silhouettes, but for the first time, what became known as the American 'sack suit' was our own signature. So, he embraced it, I feel, because it helped him to fit into a very tasteful, sophisticated side of self-expression that, everyone found appealing. I don't think he was trying to cross over by any means, but I think he understood the power of it, and it was a crisp, clean look and he fit right into it. But as he evolved through the different eras, he was embracing the cutting edge of style, just as he was purveying the cutting edge of music. For him to travel the world and not be inspired by Asian designers, or European designers, which could be a little wacky, would not be unheard of, especially for someone who at that time, was a global superstar. You can't put expectations of a pedestrian on a 'pop star'. So yeah, he started in a very polished, pedestrian way, but he's in show business, he's a star and people expect a show, not only in the music, but in performance. So, I'm not surprised that he didn't want to show that he was losing his hair, the same way that Michael Jackson or any other star.

For someone like Miles Davis, where the music was really paramount, the clothing was really his way to express himself, to complement or to clash with it in a funky way and that's what jazz is all about. Some of those notes that are slightly off-key sound the most beautiful, sometimes you expect a beautiful note to end the song, but the best jazz musicians, like Miles or Dizzy, would give an almost out of tune note at the very end and just leave you wanting more, feeling the romance of a song that wasn't quite perfect or quite symmetrical, that has verve to it and kind of a flippant feel to it.

What do you think makes Miles Davis a fashion icon even more than twenty years after his death?

He wasn't looking to be one. As a culture, we weren't spotlighting style and fashion the way we do today. For instance, people watch the red-carpet commentary for the big awards shows with the same interest that they watch sports events in this day and age. Sometimes the red carpet is more exciting than the event it's preceding. In Miles's heyday, he was someone who had a more poignant, individual personal style that came alive at a time when people really didn't write stories around it. He wasn't trying to spin off a line of clothes, or a cologne or a line of shoes that were inspired by him, there was no commerce attached to it, which gave him an authenticity that's very different from today.

So I think when magazines like Esquire and GQ are looking through the annals of history of who really shaped style and changed the trajectory of style, you have to give him credit for that because 1: he brought a certain swagger to it that only a man of color could, 2: it was really a compliment to his first love, which was the music, and finally, again, it was nothing commercial for him. Whether people liked it or not, whether it was classic in the early days or edgy and avant-garde in his later years, he didn't care if he made a list or not. It was his own personal expression. The same way today you see Black men, whether they are preachers, politicians, athletes or businessmen, you name it, they will choose a look, a shoe a pocket square that isn't something that you would see in GQ each month. That's that lineage of who we are, that's our self-expression, we don't need the approval of the masses or the establishment. Miles Davis is very much a public side of that same spirit.

Is there a particular era of Miles's style that appeals to you the most?

When I think about those images of him, those easy images, where he's wearing a simple, crisp, button-down and a pair of high waisted pleated pants. There's an image of him leaning on a piece of glass, with rolled-up sleeves and high-waisted pleated pants, I'm assuming that was the fifties? That moment was great. It's so timeless, that image could be on the cover of a magazine today or in an ad campaign, like The Gap did in the eighties and nineties. There's something so timeless and elegant that you can't put a date stamp on it. He didn't have a high-top fade; it was nothing that signified a particular era or time. Then he'd add a scarf or a cardigan sweater, very much the same look that you might see someone like Frank Sinatra wearing, but it was really unique to Miles's look as a Black man to give it that little extra soul that set it apart.

Is there any recommendation you would offer to a guy, young or old who is trying to find the style that is peculiar to him? Is there anything from Miles Davis's fashion canon that would be applicable?

If you want to achieve that classic Miles look, especially from my favorite era, that mid-century era, keep in mind what I always say: "less is modern". What I mean is that there is an understated elegance, a purity, a simplicity to his choices that are more about taking off than adding on. The power and restraint that he showed of knowing that a beautiful button-down shirt in a gorgeous fabric, paired with perfectly tailored pants with the ideal break at the cuff was all he needed to go along with a shined loafer and then he stopped there. Most men today tend to add on or stack on, thinking that it makes for a better ensemble when knowing when to stop is what makes it elegant and understated.

Do you have a favorite Miles Davis album?

(Chuckles) I guess it would have to be the most cliché, 'Kind of Blue'. I mean you can't get around it. As much as everyone tries to find something different or obscure, the butter, flour, sugar of his collection would have to be that album. You can play it at a brunch, a long drive up the coast, you can play it at a cocktail party in any country and everyone would get it, you know? It fits any mood that you were feeling.

How would you describe Miles Davis in a single word?

'Smooth'. That reps the music, the clothes, his posture, his legacy. I'm sure there were ups and downs with the marriages, but there was no scandal that ripped his legacy apart. He had some ups and downs with his image and his wardrobe, but for the most part he had a smooth look about him. There's an art to being smooth, and as much as it has been clowned in our community, that smooth machismo thing, he did it in a way that wasn't clownish.

Reggie Hudlin is a renaissance man. Writer ('The Black Panther'), director ('House Party', 'Boomerang'), producer ('Django Unchained') comic book publisher (Milestone Media), are just a few of his long list of achievements. Growing up in East St. Louis, Illinois, Hudlin has long been impacted by the name 'Miles Davis'. An insightful social commentator with a particular affinity for pop culture, Reggie offers some thoughtful insights on his Midwestern homeboy.

What's your first memory of Miles Davis?

I guess it's the album cover, with saturated red light ('round About Midnight). It's not a memory of hearing him, but seeing him, which looked as adult as it sounded (laughs)! As kids, you get to hear not just the music that your peers are playing, but you get to hear music six or seven years beyond you, from your older siblings. And then, my parents were real music heads, and there was a lot of playing and listening in our household.

Duke Ellington, Louie Armstrong, Nancy Wilson, those are the things I got first. My dad was a real Count Basie, Duke Ellington man. He was into jazz you danced to. So, he had that album. I never heard him play it, but it was there, as a presence in our house, and it was intimidating.

Why?

It told you. It was truth in advertising! And then, we knew about Miles Davis, because Mrs. Davis taught third grade at the local elementary school. Everyone knew Mrs. Davis was tough, Mrs. Davis was 'ruler on the knuckle', kind of teacher. She was a beautiful woman. She was striking. She taught at Alta Sita grade school, which was three blocks away from my house.

He was born in Alton Illinois. Were you were born close by?

I was born in Centerville, but I grew up in East St. Louis. Jo Davis, one of his nephews, he and I were in high school together. The Davis family, even long after he had left, still had a presence in town. I remember after I left for college, they dedicated one of the local elementary schools to Miles, and Miles and Cicely (Tyson) went back for that. I remember the picture in the local paper of him in East St. Louis, which literally looked like an alien had landed in some rural Black town! Leather, black big shoulder pads, slicked-back hair, wrapped around shades, the whole nine. Cicely was beautiful and elegant. She was like the humanizing element to the alien.

So how would you say your connection to Miles developed?

Kind of Blue. I got to him through the sidemen first. Weather Report, that *Mr. Gone* album, *Heavy Weather* and all that stuff. It was challenging, but I loved it. But wait a minute: all these guys, all these bad cats came from Miles. Everything in life keeps pointing back to this dude, this mountain that you have to climb. So, you start with *Kind of Blue* and you start working your way through. Even though I'm not listening to that much Miles, I'm reading about Miles. The *Bitches Brew* album cover, my cool older cousins, they all had it, and it was the same artist who did the Santana *Abraxas* album cover, so you go, 'well, he was the coolest artist in the game, with the coolest covers in the game', and you're like 'wow, I want to listen to that', but when they put it on, you're like 'whoa!!!' You just couldn't hang! I'm attracted to this...and this is where style counts: we've just been talking about album covers! We haven't even talked about the music yet! These album covers keep seducing me! How can I get down with what this is?!

Finally, I start working my way through. And I start appreciating it. I'm still trying to get my arms around the sextet stuff, that stuff is really ambitious and challenging to me. But the joy is, as a guy who just consumes culture at a really, really fast rate, it's great to know that there's a meal in the refrigerator. There's no rush! I've got another thirty, forty years to work my way through this stuff.

He did the *Tutu* album when he switched to Warner Bros. That was a great, great thing to introduce him to a whole new generation. And it was a great record. I still love that record. Suddenly he was available and accessible. He did that video with Spike (Lee) and this is when we were all coming up in the film game. It was an exciting period.

I hired Marcus Miller to score *House Party*, my first film. By talking with Marcus and hearing Miles stories, I'm getting closer and closer to the man. So, *House Party* comes out and I'm working with a publicist who also represents Miles. We just finished a press event and she went to a phone on the corner, this was pre-cell phone. She said 'I have to call Miles Davis.

If he lets you, would you want to meet him?' She talks to him and says you can go up for fifteen minutes. I said, 'I'll take it!'

We leave the press event and go to his place in Metropolitan Tower, next to the Russian Tea Room. He opens the door and I completely break cool. There's no cool in my opening line. 'I'm from East St. Louis!' He goes (whispering) 'I know. My people know your people'. And he invites me in. The living room is dominated by this huge canvas on the floor. It's too tall, so he had to lay it on the floor to paint. I'd never seen an artist work that way. We start talking about the art and he shows me this book of sketches that he has. And it comes out that he wants to design a stage that looks like his art. We're talking about it and finally I get to the point where I have to leave for a TV appearance that I have to do. My publicist calls me later and says, 'that was amazing. I've never seen Miles take to anyone that he just met, like that.' The funny story is that the TV appearance I went to do was live, so everybody in the other room (at Miles' home) turned it on and said, 'hey Miles look, it's Reggie, he's on TV'. Miles said, 'fuck that nigger! That nigger was just here! Fuck that nigger (laughs)!'

A month or so passes, I get this phone call, he calls and says 'Miles Davis'. I can't believe Miles Davis is calling my house. And he remembers the conversation we were having about the stage. He was doing this big show in Paris and he wanted my help in designing the stage. He had some very specific requirements about the stage. I hang up the phone and can't believe the conversation I just had. Fortunately, my girlfriend at the time managed fashion designers, so she had a sense of fabric and design. My best friend from childhood who's an engineer, he truly understood Miles Davis' music. He plays saxophone in addition to being a left brain/right brain genius.

We go to dinner and I say, 'I need you two to help me figure this out'. Over the course of the dinner we actually figure out the staging. I'm super excited. I'm calling and calling and calling, and I can't get Miles on the phone. And that was that (laughs)!

Really?

Whatever impulse he had, it went away. I saw him at a birthday party at the Boathouse years later. I reintroduced myself and he clearly had no idea who I was. But I had it! I had a story I could tell you!

Do you have a favorite era of Miles?

I'm gonna cherry-pick around. *Kind of Blue* is a beast of a record. That and *Tutu* are the two I've played the most. That *Porgy and Bess* album gets a lot of workout from me too. The accessible stuff, but that said, last year, I really started listening to *On the Corner*. I'm going in! On certain days it sounds so wonderful and so jammin' to me, and certain days, it's like 'uh oh! Wrong approach!'

Miles' sense of style, your thoughts?

First off, his sense of style is him being a complete artist. Everything was a canvas, including his clothing. Second of all, being from East St. Louis and knowing the importance of style in East St. Louis, he's being a product of his environment. One of my favorite things reading his autobiography was the importance of the stiff, starched collar and how fly that look was.

In terms of America's relation to him, it's no accident that he did an album called *Jack Johnson*. He was (one of) those pioneering Black men, who felt no obligation to smile and had no problem expressing their full masculinity. In an environment where being assertive is seen to be aggressive when you act light a human being, you're accused of being an asshole. 'No, I'm just being a man.'

So that was pioneering work because it was hard. It was physically hard, it was psychologically hard, but he was a hard man. He was built for it. I think a lot of that hardness was because he was so sensitive. He had to create this hard, hard exterior. I mean great artists, lots of time people misperceive them: 'he's an asshole, he doesn't listen to anybody...'. No, no, no, no. They're reading everything that's going on. They're completely aware of it and they're fighting to maintain their artistic integrity. And when you're as much of a visionary as he is, seeing stuff that no one else can see, you have to build out incredible body armor to pursue this journey. He had to do that.

There was that great question in *Lincoln*: Does the man make the times or does the times make the man? I once heard Bill Gates talk about it. Everyone wants to believe in that 'Great Man' theory, that this great man came forth and changed the world. But maybe the times demanded that that person exist. It's hard to know, but the point is, Miles was needed, and Miles was.

Why do you think that of all of the other outstanding jazz musicians who also had a sense of style, Miles was often seen as and referred to as 'The One'?

He was forward-thinking through different eras of style. He kept making a big impression on multiple generations. He was always a visual representation of what he sounded like. And that's good. Going back to me as a kid, I didn't hear that record, but I knew what it sounded like just from looking at it. And he always looked what he sounded like. It's good marketing, it's being a complete artist, it's everything it was.

Why in your opinion do you think that in his last few years, as his music got more accessible, Miles's look became less accessible?

I would say just the opposite: he was getting your attention. He wanted you to pay attention. 'Look at me. Listen to me'. I don't mean to sound simplistic or stereotypical, but we all like bright colors! You stop and you look. Miles could have worn beautiful, dark Armani suits and he would have been stylish as hell. But he didn't want to disappear. He wanted to pop! He was playing 'pop' music and his music popped. I don't see it as a contradiction at all. I see it as a natural extension.

The thing about Miles is that you always want him around. You always want his take on whatever era you're living in. He always has something interesting to say and express.

His impact seems to be stronger now than when he was alive. Why is that?

Miles was a capital 'A' artist who also understood branding in a way that Picasso also understood branding. He was one of those guys who held the entire equation in his head. Because he was a successful artist and businessman, he himself is literally a milestone. He is Mount Rushmore-

35

worthy. I mean, if you're going to have a musical Mount Rushmore, Chuck Berry's on it, Miles Davis is on it. He's on the very, very short list of people who represent a kind of music and a style and an era. He embodies six or seven things simultaneously and seamlessly. Art is literally vanishing, craftsmanship is vanishing, being replaced by marketing and hype. So, as a person who is the real thing, yet has all of the hooks for today's hype-driven era, of course there is a greater need for him than ever before.

If you could describe him in a single word, what would it be?

You can't describe a word with a word, but Miles is Miles. He _is_ a descriptive term. I'll just say 'Miles'. I don't even have to say 'Davis'.

1. Y

OUNG MAN WITH A HORN: 1950-1959

Jazz is like blues with a shot of heroin'.

-Miles Davis

At the end of the fifties, Miles Davis could look back and see that he was responsible for some of the most influential music in the history of jazz, some of which wasn't appreciated upon its initial release, but is now seen as groundbreaking. Ending the decade, he had to be excited about his possibilities, both personally and professionally. But in 1950, it's likely that he would have laughed if someone told him how the decade would turn out, because for Miles Davis, its start was anything but assured.

Meanwhile, America, had its own juggling act to balance. In 1950, just a few years after World War II, the US transitioned into a sort of steady state on the surface: conservatism was the word and materialism took on a new kind of prominence. Bubbling under the seemingly tranquil new decade, the Red scare was gaining steam through the exhortations of Senator Joseph P. McCarthy, the Korean War got underway and African Americans expressed their displeasure on a national scale.

The Fifties was the decade where the Civil Rights Movement started to gain traction. The vigorous demand for equal rights and fair treatment had existed since slaves were brought to America. But when African Americans returned home from fighting for their country, which led to losing their lives on foreign soil only to find that they were still considered second class citizens, there was a subtle, but noticeable shift. Blacks were less inclined to be quiet and accept ill-treatment without some form of protest. For someone like Miles, who had always been aware of and sensitive to racial discrimination, he was more than ready for the times to catch up with him, culturally and socially.

Musically, pop standards still revolved around crooners. Sinatra, Crosby and Patti Page were constantly on the charts. The big band sound faded slowly as the vocalists began to draw attention to themselves. Rock and roll was around the corner while rhythm and blues music was largely restricted to black radio stations, and thus relegated to the farthest end of the radio dial.

While America was figuring out its identity at the start of a new decade,

Miles Davis was thousands of miles away in another country experiencing the impact of a new culture on his still-developing psyche.

In late 1949, Miles went to tour Paris as part of a jazz combo. He was overwhelmed by the respect and adulation Parisian audiences gave him and the other players. The sea of white faces repeatedly showering him with love and admiration for his talent was unexpected. The idea of a majority of white patrons treating him not only as a complete human being, but also as a musical treasure, was something that Miles appreciated deeply, but he was still resentful that he had to go abroad to be given what he felt he deserved. But that didn't stop Miles from exploring his interest in French and European culture.

French art, music and dance were served up in copious amounts to Miles and he inhaled deeply. In fact, the culture of France served as an aphrodisiac, as he was almost immediately entranced by the French actress and singer Juliette Greco. They enjoyed a passionate romance, with Greco imploring Miles to stay with her in Paris. But as much as he had come to love her, New York was calling (not to mention his wife, who had by then, moved to the city, with Cheryl and son Gregory, born in 1946).

Miles reluctantly came back, but he was instantly swallowed by depression. Partially because he was back to his still oppressive homeland, and also because he was stuck in a loveless marriage and he missed Greco, Miles was more vulnerable than he had ever been, making a casual liaison he had developed in the late forties, his most prominent relationship for the first half of the fifties.

He started using drugs and the association that consumed him and largely took over his life was heroin. Miles with a little dabbling with the opiate once he was locked into the New York jazz scene, but his addiction took full flight and sent him spiraling for several years. Throughout his struggle with addiction he never stopped playing even when the addition hurt and almost ruined his musicianship. He started pimping in order to make enough money to keep up with the drugs, and even the birth of his son Miles IV in 1950, couldn't motivate him to get the monkey off of his back.

Miles hit a low, but he was not yet at rock bottom when he was busted for possession while on tour with Billy Eckstine on tour in Los Angeles. There was a slight bright side, prior to the bust he had the opportunity to play with Billie Holiday, so after his arrest, he reconnected and stayed with Dexter Gordon while awaiting trial. Miles' drug bust flew past the eyes of the media, so the majority of the public knew nothing about it until Cab Calloway outed him in a *Down Beat* magazine interview. Miles never forgave Calloway for that betrayal.

But even in the throes of addiction, Miles kept at it, back in New York, recording with Charlie Parker for Verve Records, then cutting tracks for competitor Prestige Records on the same day! He also met and hired John Coltrane in 1952. Pianist Ahmad Jamal's use of space captivated him and helped him sever his connection to bebop jazz. And one of the most important musical discoveries of his career was the adoption of the Harmon mute, which helped him create a relaxed sound and provided him with the level of intimacy that all trumpet players since have strived to emulate. Jazz was still his muse, but heroin had become the mistress that wouldn't let him go. Even the arrival of Dr. Davis in New York, on a mission to take his son home and get him clean, wasn't enough to (literally) move the needle.

As you might imagine, clothes and style were low priorities for Miles Davis during this period. To be clear, until he hit rock bottom, he still cut a dashing figure, as photos show him in rollneck sweaters, gray flannels and beautiful woolen suits. Nonetheless, fashion took a back seat, especially since he spent most of if not all his money on drugs.

But the American male had made some adjustments in the meantime. While the late forties were a return to prosperity with bigger, more dramatic styles for both men and women, the fifties turned down the volume, which made men's fashion more subdued at the time. What became known as the businessman's look was the new order of the day. The sack suit, soft shoulders, shorter jacket, no cut in the body was the go-to look for much of white-collar America. Its most popular look was the name of a film *The Man in the Gray Flannel Suit* (1956), starring Gregory Peck.

Whether it was gray, dark blue or brown, the new look reflected the conservatism that was sweeping the country. Pants were shorter, ties were skinnier and the bon vivant of the Mr. B collar was replaced by a smaller, simpler neckline. The threat of the Cold War and the dawning realization of the power of nuclear weaponry cast a pall over lifestyle items often known for their frivolousness. As mens-fashion.lovetoknow.com observed, 'Everyone wanted to look like a good American, which meant they all looked alike'.

However, African American men continued to add a personal touch to their style to give it a special flair. Shirts with embroidery, stylish hats that often matched a shirt and pair of pants added casual glamour to an everyday look. Accessories gained more importance as time went by. Rings, cufflinks, classy watches and cool belts kept the black man in style while continuing to reach for the American dream. On the national stage, men like Harry Belafonte and Sammy Davis Jr. were prime examples of the tasteful style mavens of the day.

Back in New York, Miles bottomed out and went home to St. Louis to kick his heroin addiction cold turkey. In classic fashion, with the help of his loyal father, Miles locked himself in room and went through a near crippling withdrawal period.

After he cleaned up following several brief backslides, Miles resumed recording for Prestige, which gave birth to a collection of albums that demonstrated his move from bebop to hard bop. Hard bop, as the name implies, is a more aggressive, percussive driven sound, while often using slower tempos to propel the melody. Improvisation was a part of this new sound, as was a clear connection to the blues. Among the commonly regard classics are *Dig, Bags' Groove, Walkin'* and several sessions from his time at Blue Note. To help get him back on his feet, Miles, as always, enlisted high-quality players. Art Blakey, Sonny Rollins and John Coltrane were cornerstones of several of his combos.

Having led several combos by now, Miles had become a real leader. He had clear ideas about what he wanted and how to achieve it; hence he minced no words in telling players when they weren't giving him what he needed. The days of the young man with a horn happy to be in the studio were over. Having recovered from what could have been a career-ending phase, Miles was determined to not waste time with niceties in order to get the music that he wanted.

In 1955, he had an operation to remove polyps from his larynx. The doctor ordered him not to speak for several days, but he raised his voice in an argument, resulting in the now-famous raspy whisper of a voice that most fans became with. The result of his distinctive voice and his now well-known short temper could be seen as the origins of his reputation for being difficult and surly. Prior to this period, Miles was generally described as a quiet, thoughtful guy. That description was rarely used after the fifties.

To be fair, coming out of the heroin haze with a new resolve, Miles probably felt that in order to protect himself from falling back into his old habits, he needed a defense, something that would keep him in check and in turn, keep the wrong people away from him, while still keeping the right people on their toes. When he returned to his music with a clear head, Miles was grateful that his gift hadn't left him and was determined to make the most of the second chance.

His appearance at the Newport Jazz Festival in 1955 was a resounding success and is generally cited as one of the highlights of his career. While he continued to follow his musical ideas, Miles founded what would be forever known as his 'first great quintet'. This group of young musicians strongly believed in Miles and his music and showed great range in a variety of styles. Coltrane on tenor sax was revelatory, Red Garland played piano, Paul Chambers handled the bass and Philly Joe Jones anchored on drums.

Miles let his melodic instincts come to the fore with this ensemble, playing sweet melancholy cues, which invited Coltrane to hit the heights with explosive but emotional solos. Columbia Records liked what it heard and came calling. Once Miles' contract with Prestige had been completed, he signed with Columbia, in what would be the longest recording contract of his career.

The quintet broke up in 1957 and Miles played with a variety of players until he reunited with a now drug-free Coltrane, Philly Joe Jones and several other seminal musicians, including Thelonious Monk, both of whom would be fired and replaced by Bill Evans and Jimmy Cobb. Evans's delicate style on the piano would find its way into Miles approach on the trumpet. In 1958, Miles took a quick break to marry Broadway dancer Frances Taylor.

As his creative engine continued to rev up, Miles and Gil Evans came together to start what would be known as one of the most memorable runs of adventurous, unpredictable albums ever heard in jazz.

Supported by Evans elegant arrangements, *Miles Ahead* surrounded Miles with a big band and horn section, while *Porgy and Bess*, featured songs arranged by Evans from George Gershwin's opera of the same name. They continued with the remarkable *Sketches of Spain*, featuring Miles supported by an orchestra, playing original songs and arrangements by Evans and Joaquin Rodrigo. This session was replicated on the live album, *Miles Davis at Carnegie Hall*, released in 1961.

The fifties ended for Miles Davis with a blend of highs and lows. In 1959, following the creatively satisfying experience of working shoulder to shoulder with Gil Evans on several albums that had the jazz world spinning, Miles decided to round up his sextet to concentrate on an album that would investigate his recent interest in modal music, a style that focused on one chord, instead of volatile chord changes inherent in bebop.

Miles recruited Bill Evans, who was of a like mind and could articulate modal ideas on piano. The result was the album, *Kind of Blue*, which became the definitive Miles Davis recording that went on to be the best-selling jazz album in history and a true cultural landmark. *Kind of Blue* is to jazz what *Thriller* was to pop. Books have been written on the creation of *Kind of Blue*, and its importance as a piece of American culture is so inarguable that the House of Representatives voted 409-0 to have it installed as a national treasure of the United States.

Unfortunately, everyone didn't appreciate the valuable cultural service Miles provided. In the summer of 1959, Miles and his quintet were in the midst of a stand at the legendary Birdland nightclub in New York. During a break, Miles escorted a blonde female friend to a cab. A local patrolman came up and told Miles to move. The musician protested on the grounds that he was playing in the club across the street; the club that had his name on the marquee. The policeman said he didn't care and grabbed Miles. He punched Davis in the stomach with his baton while another officer held back a gathering crowd and a third officer arrived and hit Miles in the head, causing a wound that took five stitches to close.

Miles was then taken to jail where **he** was charged with assaulting an officer, when bystanders repeatedly said that he was only defending himself. A year later he was acquitted of disorderly conduct and another year later the assault charge against him was dropped. The case was closed, but the damage had already been done. As Miles recounted in his autobiography, the incident 'changed my whole life and whole attitude again, made me feel bitter and cynical again when I was starting to feel good about the things that had changed in this country' (*autobiography, pg. 238*). Throughout the sixties his pain was heavily felt in countless interviews laced with hostility and resentment, which were all products of the problem of race relations in America. And his wife Frances, would unfortunately too often find herself on the receiving end of his fury.

But during this inexcusable incident, Frances rushed to Miles' side as he was handcuffed and led away to the police, with a furious and outraged look on his face. Photos exist of a bloody Miles with Frances, in handcuffs, with a white bandage on his head and blood on his cotton sport coat and button-down shirt. Surprisingly, even when he looked banged up and bloody, Miles Davis had style.

That particular style, minus the blood, was known as the Ivy League, another potent ingredient in the Miles Davis mystique. Complementing his explorations in music, his clothes reflected an equally curious and adventurous sensibility. Sometime shortly after his return from the fog of heroin, Miles made a sartorial shift. Having spent his first decade in New York focused primarily on music (and for a time drugs), he started his second decade by expressing himself as more than just an art or a craft, but as an individual in all of his endeavors, not only on the trumpet.

Gone were the big-shouldered, full pleated suits favored by Dexter Gordon and other prominent players. Miles embraced the idea of having his clothes fit close to his trim, boxer honed physique. On the east coast, he became a regular at the Andover Shop in Cambridge, where master tailor Charlie Davidson worked with him to find the right cut fabric and color for his suits and sport coats.

Soft shoulders and English tweed jackets with narrow lapels became Miles' regular outfit. Button-down shirt collars were the norm, memorably captured on the cover of his album *Milestones*, where a relaxed Miles rests in a chair sporting a green button-down cotton shirt with the sleeves rolled up, a nonchalant look on his face and his trumpet on his thigh, at the ready. Pants were slim, flat front affairs, often in khaki or wool. Miles loved solid colored ties and rep ties and often completed his look with Weejun loafers.

He could still dress with a flourish. In the thirty-minute CBS television special 'The World of Miles Davis', Miles is featured in a light-colored trim suit with a short jacket and a scarf tied rakishly around his neck. Checked open-neck shirts were also a favorite during this time as were the dark sunglasses he often wore. His jackets were tapered at the waist, his sleeves were slightly slanted, and pockets would often have piping. The little touches were as important to him as the fabric and fit.

Miles did not just know how to dress well; he equally knew how to accent his silhouette. The soft-shouldered, easy elegance of his posture was highlighted when he was onstage, blowing his horn. His suits would hang just so, with the jacket just a bit shorter in the back to ensure the proper drape when he played. When he wasn't blowing his horn, he would prowl the stage almost distractedly, while his outfit would gently follow its master's command. Ignoring his audience, almost daring them to leave when he played entire concerts with his back to them, Miles Davis was the master of his universe.

This period for Miles' style defines the definition of a 'perfect storm'. With the shift in music, the change in his speaking voice, the troubled drug period, the creative musical breakthroughs, the transcendent *Kind of Blue* and the tragic police beating, Miles had built a profile like no other musician in popular music. And the visual images of him during this period are themselves timeless examples of inspired photography with a subject who knew the value of mystique and branding long before it became popular. These photographs spotlight a beautiful, self-possessed, dark-skinned black man who was clearly American, but at the same time refused to be constricted by America's limitations. These were timeless images of a solitary genius at the peak of his creative powers, always impeccably dressed and clearly didn't give a damn about what you thought of him.

Young Man with a Horn
CONVOS

The Ivy League look has enjoyed a resurgence in popularity over the years, due in part to designers like Ralph Lauren and Tommy Hilfiger's reinterpretation of the classic button-down style. But the true Ivy League pedigree has continued to thrive, whether it's a part of a hot designer trend or not. **Charlie Davidson**, *owner and operator of the Andover Shop in Cambridge, Massachusetts since 1953, is one of the true keeps of the flame. At a robust 88 years of age at the time of this interview, Mr. Davidson was kind enough to talk about the days of dressing the Prince of Darkness in the cool lines of the Ivy League. I wish that you could hear his voice, it's as raspy and colorful as Miles's himself.*

So, you and Miles?

I knew Miles very well. We had a lot of mutual friends. In spite of the fact that many people say he was so difficult, he and I had a very nice time together. I met him through a jazz club. George Wien, later of Import Jazz fame, had a very good club in Boston called Storyville. All the great jazz players played there. I'd be over there every night because I loved the music so much. And I met Charlie Bourgeois (Wein's partner) and he brought the musicians who cared about clothes to the shop. In no time at all, everybody in that world was coming to my store. I made suits for all the guys in Miles's band. Miles was very, very fashion conscious, always. He'd come and sit around the shop and critique clothes that other guys were buying. He could be a wise guy in a very wonderful way.

What was his dressing like when you met him?

World War II-style. But Miles was so sharp, right away. He knew the difference, the real thing in a new approach. He was very, very perceptive, about everything. The Ivy League…that's a terrible name, but the Ivy League was cool, coming together at that time.

How did you work with him and the other musicians at the time?

The musicians never said, 'pick something out for me'. Most jazz musicians had incredibly good taste, in everything. If they were reading a book, and some of these guys would barely talk it was a damned good book. Miles would say, 'I want one of those'. He didn't ask my opinion. If it was in the store, he knew I'd make it the way he wanted it. He chose his own things. He wanted the band to wear suits, but he didn't trust their taste, so those he and I would do together.

A lot of these guys, like JJ Johnson, they had very good taste. They would be very comfortable with the stuff that I was selling. They'd say, 'oh yeah, that's great' and get whatever they wanted.

Were there any favorite pieces that you put him in?

I keep a file of all the things I've made for customers. About ten years ago, there was a Miles Davis retrospective that was going to tour across the country and Europe. They asked me if I would let them use the samples and measurements of Miles that I made. It turns out that I shouldn't have given it to them. I've never gotten them back. I didn't dream that I wouldn't get that stuff back. (Pause) He really was ahead of his time. The original Ivy League model was really quite dumpy, very casual, a natural shoulder and all of that. Miles liked it a little bit sharper. Plaid jackets, very trim trousers. He got it immediately.

How tall was he?

He was about 5'6-7". He was in between a 38 regular and a short. He was built like a lightweight boxer, rugged shoulders, pretty trim at the waist.

Was he easy to make clothes for?

Easy, but fussy. He knew exactly the length he wanted the sleeves, the length of the coat. He was a very complicated guy. Part of his image was not to talk so much about it. He was so sharp, but he didn't want to have to discuss it much. More concerned about being cool, than explaining it too much. That cool era was carried out in everything.

Do you remember your last encounter with him?

Yes, I do. It was at a jazz festival when he had gone completely over to the electric stuff. And he was wearing pretty outlandish stuff. A complete change. Many years ago, when I was being interviewed for something else for Vanity Fair, I said 'deep down, sometimes I think Miles wanted to be

Prince'. Miles wanted to be a star.

Unprovoked, Mr. Davidson told me a story Miles told him about his childhood.

When he was in the seventh grade, a kid came to school with velvet on the collar, like a chesterfield coat. When Miles went home to his mother, he said, 'I want velvet on all the collars of my jackets, or I won't go to school again.' So, his mother put velvet collars on all of his sport coats. He had it all. He really did.

If you could describe Miles Davis in one word, what would it be?

'Fascinating'. I'll tell you what he really was. One time Zoot Sims was being interviewed, and was asked, what kind of guy was Stan Getz? Zoot thought for a minute and he said, 'Stan was an interesting bunch of guys'. I don't think I could improve on that to describe Miles. Stan was very much like Miles, he could be charming, he could be a pain in the ass, but I think that's a very wonderful loving description of both of them.

FIVE QUESTIONS WITH BRYAN FERRY

*One of rock music's originals, **Bryan Ferry** has remained a major star even after the seventies, when his prog-rock band Roxy Music turned the UK music scene upside down. Lead singer and writer Ferry was majorly the brain behind shaping the band's image, using superstar models set against elegant backdrops for the band's album cover and cultivating an image of the elegantly libertine front man. Ferry has long been regarded as one of the world's best-dressed men, and counts being named to the International Best-Dressed List Hall of Fame in 2009 with other inductees like Fred Astaire, Pierre Cardin and Douglas Fairbanks, Jr.*

In an interview a few years ago, Bryan Ferry named Miles Davis as one of his personal heroes. As an icon who wears his own style as effortlessly as his hero, Bryan Ferry graciously consented to a brief interview here where he considers the influence of Miles.

Do you remember the first time you experienced Miles Davis? What did it feel like?

One of the first records I bought (in 1956) was an EP of The Charlie Parker Quintet, which featured Miles Davis as the second lead. This record became a kind of talisman for me and I knew it so well I memorised all the solos, both by Charlie Parker and Miles. I thought they were the perfect foil for one another, with Parker's fluid lines beautifully counter-balanced by Davis's cool and cloaked introspective statements. I've never heard a record since that meant so much to me.

Did you ever see him live?

I have never seen him perform live. The closest I have got to him is working with the bass player Marcus Miller on several of my albums. Marcus, of course, played with Miles towards the end of his career.

Like you, Miles Davis is considered one of the great male fashion icons of the last five decades. What is it about his personal style that makes him so compelling?

I was very taken by those early photographs of him playing alongside Charlie Parker and I even have one of those pictures on the wall of my recording studio in London, which gives me great inspiration. Sartorially, the look of be-bop perfectly matched the music and the sharp suit, shirt and tie look has been pretty much my way of dressing for most of my life.

What, if any, effect did his sartorial and musical concepts have on the way you developed your image and/or music?

The balance of passion and reason on those four tracks I mentioned set the pattern for my own career. (Incidentally, these tracks 'Au Privave', 'KC Blues', 'Star Eyes' and 'She Rote', were all recorded I believe in New York City in 1951.

It seems that you and Miles evolved in opposite directions, as it pertains to fashion. As a member of Roxy Music, you started out with flamboyant outfits that ultimately gave way to a more refined, elegant, yet personalized style. Miles, on the other hand, started out stately, with smartly tailored suits and ultimately, particularly in the last decade of his life, he turned to more garish, idiosyncratic outfits, whether onstage or off. What would you say about your personal transition and what you make of Miles' later evolution?

I don't think it's of much consequence one way or the other. Sometimes people get bored with how they look and want a change. It goes without saying that I prefer Miles' earlier more sober appearance, which seemed to match the well-measured quality of his playing. In his later career I think he was perhaps trying too hard to appeal to a newer, younger audience.

If you could describe Miles Davis in a single word, what would it be?

It seems rather obvious, but I would have to say… 'cool'.

Monica Miller *is an associate professor of English at Barnard College, a private women's liberal arts college in New York City. Professor Miller specializes in African American and American literature and culture. She's also the author of the award-winning book, Slaves to Fashion: Black Dandyism and the Styling of Black Diasporic Identity. In her book, Professor Miller does an historical examination of the style of the black dandy in America. What is a black dandy and how does it relate to Miles Davis, you probably ask? Read on.*

How would you define a Dandy?

In my book *Slaves to Fashion*, I use two definitions of "dandy" to capture the totality of what I think the word means and what it can do. The first is an "official" definition from the *Oxford English Dictionary*: a dandy is one who "*studies* above everything else to dress elegantly and fashionably" (18th century). This definition of sartorial action is in contrast to that of a "fop," who is one "foolishly attentive to and vain of his appearance, dress or manners" (from the 15th century). To me, the word "dandy" implies a certain kind of intentionality, a knowingness about the potential power of clothing, style, self-presentation. There is nothing "foolish" about being a dandy, as it is often a choice, a vocation, a strategy.

The second definition that I am attentive to highlights the performative nature of a dandy figure: I define dandies as figures who through clothing, gesture *and* wit (all three) are trying to say something about representation (as men, as racialized figures), social position, or political possibilities through their sartorial play. Dandyism is often an ironic gesture or pose, designed to critique the status quo.

How does that definition expand or change when you add 'Black' to?

Adding the adjective "black" to "dandy" places it in a particular historical-political context that is consequential for thinking about black identity, representation and the origins of black aesthetic practices. In my research "black dandyism" is a phenomenon that begins with the advent of slavery and imperialism; it has been one of the ways in which power relations between black and white have been visualized and deconstructed.

As I mention in my book, while slavery manifested differently in different locations in what has come to be known as the black diaspora, a common occurrence for all slaves was the issuance of a new set of clothes upon arrival in the so-called New World. Black people understood, from this moment, that clothing was a means of expressing power; denial of proper clothing, of changes of clothes, of comfortable fabrics, of decoration and other modes of individualization, metaphorically mirrored the degraded and officially powerless political position of slaves. Wearing clothing "out of your station," aspiring to comfort, accessorizing a plain dress with a ribbon or colorful buttons, accumulating "fancy" versus functional clothing—these small gestures were also ways in which black people made bids for actual and psychological freedom. Black dandyism starts in these very material and minute gestures. By the late 18th and 19th centuries in England and in the Americas, when slaving economies are more fully developed, clothing absolutely becomes a major point of contention between slave and master, and slave and free blacks. Masters give slaves discarded fancy clothing; slaves use this clothing in festivals designed to mock authority. Some slaves in England are dressed to the nines by their masters and used as items of conspicuous consumption; some of these slaves take advantage of their social position to explicitly and implicitly argue for their humanity as they master and mock modes of aristocratic living. Some slaves escape bondage by putting on better clothes and pretending to be free; they acquire this clothing from underground second-hand clothing circuits in Northern American cities. Still other slaves are punished for insubordination by being displayed in a public setting while being inadequately clothed; laws are passed in New Orleans and Charleston, South Carolina, against the "gifting" of fancy clothing to, in particular, black women who are the concubines/lovers of their masters. Manipulation of the relationship between clothing, identity, and power, dandyism affords black people an opportunity to display their knowledge of how much "image" matters. Dandyism made it possible for some blacks to dress their way from slavery/oppression to freedom, to turn "slaves" into "selves," to re-style given categories of identity.

Would you mind mentioning some notable Black dandies?

In the African American tradition, black dandies are everywhere and dandyism or "fancy dress" has always been a part of black public culture. If

I look back into history, I think about Frederick Douglass, who may not have been a dandy per se, but was certainly a man who understood the power of image and the way in which a black man can articulate claims on humanity through the power of his rhetoric and a good suit. Douglass' portraits are a very interesting study in dignified self-presentation; they are clearly designed to refute stereotypes about black male unfitness for freedom and citizenship.

WEB Du Bois and his self-fashioning is a similar case; in the 1910s and 1920s, Du Bois was one of the sharpest dressers in Harlem. As one of the leaders of the fight for black civil rights, Du Bois knew that he needed to "look right" for the job. He, like other black elites and even regular folks at the time, was also enjoying what it meant to dress up not only in the service of civil rights, but also for pleasure. The Great Migration, which populated black urban centers like New York, Detroit and Chicago, created places that, in the early 20th century, were those in which black people dressed to impress each other, where flamboyant clothing often indicated new and outsize ideas about personal and racial possibility.

The Harlem Renaissance also gave us black entertainers for whom dandyism was a definite part of their appeal: singers and musicians have often been the black folks who have pushed boundaries. They are aspirational figures who visualize new or alternative ways of being black, masculine, feminine, straight/gay, working/middle class. A list would include: Duke Ellington, Cab Calloway, the Nichols Brothers, Gladys Bentley, Sammy Davis Jr., much of Motown (including the Supremes), Jimmy Hendrix, Sylvester, Prince, Andre 3000 of Outkast, Pharrell, sometimes Kanye West. And Miles Davis, of course.

When you look at Miles Davis, what do you see?

When I look at Miles Davis, especially in his Brooks Brothers period, I see a black man provoking a discussion, both with his music or art practice, as well as his sartorial practice. As the son of well-to-do Midwestern black family, Davis had certainly been ingrained with what is known in black culture as the "culture of respectability," a social tenet that dictates that black people must always put their best foot forward, be and look dignified and respectable. A class-based reform program that materializes Du Bois's "Talented Tenth" philosophy (that educated and accomplished blacks must "lift up" the black masses), the politics of respectability meant that black folk had to look deserving of the rights and responsibilities of citizenship. When I see Davis in a Brooks Brothers suit or even a freshly-pressed pair of khakis and an immaculate white button-down shirt, I see a man claiming his rightful "class" position (associated with Ivy League whites at the time) while at the same time confounding white expectations of his class position based on his racial identity. Additionally, he's wearing this "campus" garb on a jazz stage, a pace of entertainment previously associated with "low culture" and often, clubs on the edge of respectability. Miles on stage at this time was designed to signal that he was an artist, educated at Julliard, taking care of business on stage. Davis was, to extend the metaphor, "schooling" people with the combination of his music and look; he did, in fact, "*study* above everything else to dress elegantly and fashionably" for very specific reasons. Miles Davis' fashion choices were anything but capricious, as they were designed by him to be challenging of expectations. His music was meant to make you listen; his fashion was designed to make you look.

Would you consider Miles Davis a Black Dandy? Why so?

As mentioned above, what is most interesting to me in terms of Davis' choice of clothing during his "Cool" period and afterwards was that it was not, for example, "fancy" clothing, ex. variations on a tuxedo or morning suit, but rather "casual" clothing that was, at the time, being elevated to "fashion." While this may have happened most visibly in terms of the Ivy League look—Brooks Brothers, khaki, rep ties, letter sweaters, later slim(mer) suits, etc.—this casual fashion movement actually had another impetus: the return of soldiers from WWII. Jeans and "work clothes" like khakis were becoming popular for the elite and everybody else. What I like about Miles Davis' style during this era is that it is multiply-significant. On the one hand, he dresses as part of the trend; but the trend has multiple origins: one elite, one working class, and the other black, in that "dressing up for the job," or a disciplined, dignified self-presentation was expected for professional black people. Davis' style then is dandy-ish in that it has a knowingness about it (and an irony); he is communicating that he knows what expectations are of professional blacks, of jazz musicians, of stylish young men of the time. He is witty in his style, signifying on multiple expectations, playing with them all.

In your book, you wrote about dandyism being a form of performance. Would you care to explain what you mean in general and as it might pertain to Miles Davis in particular?

In its most progressive or positive form, dandyism allows its practitioners to "perform" or imaginatively access different identities, sometimes aspirational identities, more avant-garde identities, more inclusive identities. A much more consequential game of "dress-up," dandyism makes it possible for people to expand the definition of what they are or who they can be. For example, fashion historians have noted that some of the first noteworthy European dandies did not hail from the aristocracy or even the wealthy merchant class, instead they were working to middle-class men who adopted a different style of dress from that of the masculine "norm." This new style caused people to ask questions about who they were, what they did— the curiosity gave them a form of cultural capital that they did not have access to without actual money. A man in a tuxedo has the same effect; you have no idea where he comes from, but you ascribe a certain purposefulness, elegance and sophistication to the man in that particular "elite" uniform. Dandyism— the play with "fancy" or elite clothing in an ironic and knowing way— can provoke questions about "proper" masculine presentation, about sexual orientation, about what counts as "beauty." In terms of Miles Davis, I do think, especially as he matured, he was very interested in breaking boundaries and pushing perceived limitations, both musically and in terms of his image. He wanted first to be cool and then maybe mysterious and then, perhaps, of the future. His emerging and boundary-defying style (I'm thinking of the use of metallic fabric and the sophisticated Sun-Ra vibe he had going in the 1980s in particular) reflected this, as much as his sound.

Miles was a fashion trendsetter throughout his life, possibly peaking in the 50s through mid-sixties. Once he crossed over into electric music, his style got more and more flamboyant, possibly one of the most extreme versions of the dandy to that time. Weaves, then wigs, cowboy boots, genie pants, oversized silk shirts with heavily padded jackets; what, if anything, does his sartorial evolution suggest to you and how did his personal style reflect the black Diaspora?

As a member of the black Diaspora, Miles Davis, like all black people, lived within a representational conundrum: on the one hand, he came from a group of people with an extremely rich aesthetic drive, known for the construction, deconstruction and reassembly of aesthetic form (what we might think of as a kind of artistic wit); on the other hand he and other blacks were subjected to a representational regime that was designed to arrest that originality, flatten it out, stereotype it and the people who used it/were constituted by it. So, Davis, like many others, used Diaspora symbols and traditions as the essence of his art and by continually remaking those traditions and re-presenting them, he gestured at escaping the stereotyping. He did this at the level of both music and self-presentation: as mentioned above, he signified on a white aesthetic form (Ivy style) while also claiming it as black professional style. In his later years, he also experimented with a more "African" sense of pattern and color in his clothing. As such, he was identifying with his heritage, but never expected or wanted that identification to be static. He was always, until the very end, moving himself, his sound and his look along, always hoping to get to an unexpected, anticipated place (weaves, then wigs, cowboy boots, genie pants, oversized silk shirts with heavily padded jackets!)

3. MILES AHEAD: 1960-1966

'Everything I do, I got a reason.'

-Miles Davis, 1962

In what would later be referred to as one of the most tumultuous decades of the twentieth century, Miles Davis would begin 1960 dealing with his own form of upheaval. He was newly married, enjoying a level of popularity unprecedented by a jazz performer, especially for a black man, Miles had reached both a creative and commercial summit that for the first time, found him comfortable and seemingly stagnant.

But Miles had impacted the mainstream greatly. His tours sold out everywhere, he displaced Louis Armstrong as trumpeter of the year in the *Melody Maker* magazine poll; he was named one of *GQ* magazine's best-dressed men, a title he would two years later get from.

In the late fifties and early sixties, Italian culture was making its presence felt, via popular films like *La Dolce Vita* (translation: 'the sweet life') and suave Italian movie stars like the charismatic Marcello Mastroianni and the gorgeous Sophia Loren. International businessmen like Fiat automotive CEO Gianni Agnelli also promoted a casual but elegant style. In fact, Agnelli's individualistic approach to clothes is almost as revered as Miles' personal style.

During his tours of Europe and his restless search for the next 'thing', Miles was likely exposed to and attracted to the rule-breaking style of most Italian men: loafers with suits, unbuttoned collars on a button-down shirt, wearing watches on a shirt or jacket sleeve and close-fitting, well-tailored black suits with sunglasses. "Americans didn't live the 1950s and 60s like we did", said designer Massimo Pombo in an interview about Italian men's fashion for the Wall Street Journal. "In Italy, there was this extreme joie de vivre. It was poetic, extravagant and the extreme beauty and decadence inspired amazing garments". Ever ahead of the pack, somewhere in the sixties Miles segued from his iconic Ivy League look to a more continental style, drawing heavily on the elegant severely tailored, slim-cut Italian look.

His style was such that his onstage and offstage outfits were included in his concert press releases. Descriptions include a one-button beige pongee suit, a pink seersucker jacket and handmade doeskin loafers. *Downbeat* magazine observed in 1960 that Miles was so fashion-forward that he was modeling what they often referred to as 'what the well-dressed man will wear next year'.

Miles' popularity was appreciated by other non-musical entertainers. Superstars from other media populated his concerts regularly. It wasn't uncommon to see Paul Newman, Steve McQueen, Marlon Brando or Marilyn Monroe at a Miles Davis show. But Miles' behavior towards his 'civilian' audience, while possibly understood by his peers, bred resentment from the press and fans, which nonetheless didn't seem to bother him as he never offered them anything more than his music. He bought a five-story Russian Orthodox church on the upper west side of Manhattan and remodeled it, removing all corners and rough edges, installing a gym, rooms for his kids, a music room and other personal touches. He rented out the top two floors and lived with his family on the first three stories. His continuing interest in cars got faster and more exotic, as the Ferrari became his automotive trademark.

Miles started the new decade heading back to Europe for a tour with his band. John Coltrane had been itching to carve out his own musical direction, but Miles was able to talk the reluctant Coltrane into putting his personal passion project on hold for one final run. The tour was a successful one, but Coltrane finally decided it was time to leave when they returned to the States, and he did. As Miles worked on finding a new approach that would lead him to a creative breakthrough, the recession of 1961 was already hitting hard. Many jazz clubs were closing their doors permanently due to poor audience attendance and their inability to pay performers the rates they had become accustomed to. This led to many musicians being forced to leave the business in search of a steadier paycheck. While this didn't hit Miles nearly as hard as most of his peers, this financial reality added to an already challenging period for the dissatisfied bandleader.

Stymied without Coltrane, in 1961, Miles brought in Hank Mobley to fill in during the recording of what would become the *Someday My Prince Will Come* album, which featured Mrs. Miles Davis on the cover for the first of her three album cover appearances. Miles said that he'd never seen a black woman on the cover of an album as a model, so he enlisted Frances to add her graceful elegance to the project.

Where an album was usually recorded in a single session, *Someday My Prince Will Come* took three sessions to record. When Miles was unhappy with Mobley's performance on the title track, he reached out to John Coltrane, who came to the studio and saved the day, while also taking Mobley's place on the track, *Teo*. This was the first studio recording with the recording quintet in more than two years and it would be another two before Miles did it again.

The physical maladies that he had been fighting for years intensified and his body began to betray him. He was in a lot of pain, but for the most part he kept this to himself. He suffered an almost constant pain in his left leg, coupled with numbness and body aches. Sickle cell anemia, a blood disease that affects 1 in 500 blacks in America, had taken root in his joints. Rather than let his audience in on all the pain he was feeling, Miles would leave the stage mid-performance to tend to his ailments, leaving the crowds to come to their own conclusions.

Exercise had helped him in the past to stave off the effects of the disease. Boxing regularly helped his blood circulation and relaxed his joints. At 36 however, he realized his was body failing him more. In a search for relief, he turned to pain killers, alcohol and cocaine.

In 1962, Miles Davis participated in the very first *Playboy* magazine interview. Conducted by Alex Haley, Miles spoke with a ferocity never before expressed without hesitation by an internationally known black entertainer. Miles' view on race, music and the differences between Europe and America was startling and laid the foundation for a number of the myths that surround him to this day.

Never one to bite his tongue, Miles unleashed years of resentment at both the treatment of black people in general and himself in particular, without mincing words. Did the brutal police abuse that he suffered in 1959 contribute to his fury? Probably. Was the warm reception he received in Europe a fan that flamed his resentment when he came back to America and was met by the same racism as when he left? Probably. But he made it clear that he was a proud black man who was aware of his talent and he made it clear that all he wanted was respect for himself and his people.

"The only white people I don't like are the prejudiced white people. Those the shoe doesn't fit, well, they don't wear it. I don't like the white people that show me they can't understand that not just the Negroes, but the Chinese and Puerto Ricans and any other races that isn't white, should be given dignity and respect like everybody else." *(Playboy interview, 1962)*

While trying to figure out how to move forward musically, Miles continued working with Gil Evans, flirting with the then-popular Brazilian Bossa Nova sound, resulting in the unfinished and unsatisfying *Quiet Nights* album. With only 32 minutes of unfocused, unsettled music, neither Miles nor Gil admitted that the album was complete, let alone successful. When Columbia released it without consulting either of them, it caused a big rift between Miles and producer Teo Macero, which led to the trumpeter ricing out Macero and refusing to speak to him for nearly three years.

More successful was a benefit concert at Carnegie Hall with Evans and his orchestra, commonly regarded as one of the most transcendent performances of Miles' career. Even the disrupting presence of Max Roach, who came to the front of the stage to protest the concert on ill-defined political grounds, couldn't derail what is considered to this day, one of the all-time great concert performances. During this time, he took the quintet, minus Coltrane, to the Black Hawk in San Francisco and released a well-received, two-volume live album. The album is notable for a relaxed performance from the band as well as longer than usual solos from Miles during the stand.

The sudden death of his father in 1962 cut Miles deeply like a knife. Following an accident where his car was struck by a train, the elder Davis was no longer able to maintain his dental practice, but carried on stoically, keeping his distress to himself. Being someone who didn't know how to deal with funerals, Miles didn't attend his father's service, which was said to be one of the largest funerals ever held for a black man in St. Louis. Miles came to regret his decision for the rest of his life. The death of his mother in 1964 couldn't get him to shake his superstition about the end of life, so Frances attended the funeral on his behalf, adding more guilt to his already troubled conscience.

Musically, he continued to flounder, never having totally recovered his bearings after Coltrane broke away. In addition to the musical chairs of his saxophone slot, the rhythm section of Wynton Kelly, Paul Chambers and Jimmy Cobb left for good. But what could have been a disaster somehow turned around and became a source of creative inspiration for the Trumpeter. The musical exodus shook Miles out of his doldrums, and he set about the business of putting together a new quintet. But it was a long process that wouldn't happen overnight. Always picky about his musicians, Miles tried and tested a number of different players before he found the perfect fit.

He brought in musicians more than a decade younger than himself: Detroit bassist Ron Carter was 25 when he joined the band, pianist Herbie Hancock was 23 and a variety of sax players with George Coleman holding down the sax role until the later arrival of Wayne Shorter. But the real sparkplug of the new band was 17-year old drummer, Tony Williams. Williams' energy and enthusiasm rubbed off on Miles. His unabashed love of his elder as well as his preternatural skill resulted in Miles singing the praises of his young drummer to anyone who would listen. Perhaps the most striking show of Miles' regard for Williams was his inclusion of *Milestones* to the concert set list, largely because of Williams' love for the tune.

Once assembled, the new quintet's first recording in May 1963, was *Seven Steps to Heaven*. He initially recorded the album in California with a different group of musicians. Unhappy with the result, when he returned to New York, he re-recorded the entire album with what would be the bulk of his permanent quintet for the next six years. This would be his last studio recording until 1965.

Even though he wasn't in the studio, Miles was constantly touring, and Columbia was capturing many of the shows for possible future release. He successfully toured in Europe, where he released *Miles Davis Quintet: Live at Antibes* and *Miles Davis in Europe in 1964*. Returning stateside, the band continued to play live, gelling, led by the blistering pace set by Williams and Carter. This unit peaked during a performance at the NY Philharmonic, where George Coleman laid down some of his most inspired and confident playing. However, he left the band shortly after that, citing a variety of reasons: Miles' health, slow payments and doubt about the band's musical direction.

Following a brief replacement by Sam Rivers, the time was finally right for

Miles to hire Wayne Shorter, who had resigned from the Jazz Messengers. He got the call ('you got two eyes, come be in the band', Shorter remembers Miles saying), had a tuxedo made and flew to LA to perform with the band at the Hollywood Bowl, with no rehearsal.

Once this 'second great quintet' was assembled, they remain together for four years, which they resulted in six albums from 1965-68: *ESP* (65), *Miles Smiles* (66), *Sorcerer* and *Nefertiti* featuring future Mrs. Miles Davis, actress Cicely Tyson on the cover(67) and *Miles in the Sky* and *Kilimanjaro* (the latter featuring yet another soon to be Mrs. Miles Davis, singer Betty Mabry on the cover) both released in 1968.

While Miles was enthused about his latest group, there were reoccurring pauses, due to his inconsistent health, drug and alcohol abuse and a broken leg in August 1964. In 1965 he had hip socket surgery that failed, requiring a second operation, putting him out of commission for several months. Miles resumed work in November of 1965, doing shows in Philadelphia, performing with the band in nearby towns like Detroit and Washington. He also had to come to terms with the reality of Frances filing for divorce. He continued to work on more orchestral projects with Gil Evans that were never finished, nor released.

But the quintet that he put together eased his most important concern, the music. This ensemble rivals the great bands that he'd previously assembled, in some cases surpassing them. The quest for deeper exploration was one that all five members eagerly pursued, resulting in music that was alive and pulsing with creativity and energy while the chant of 'jazz is dead' grew louder. Many artists left the US for Europe and Japan, where the genre still thrived and was still regarded with respect. Others, who weren't so lucky, left the music business entirely. Rock and roll was becoming the order of the day, yet the battered, but not beaten Miles was gearing up to meet the challenge head-on, whether his audience was ready or not.

Miles Ahead
CONVOS

*It's easy to see why Miles Davis was mesmerized by the woman who would become his first wife. I had a series of conversations with **Frances Davis** (before she made her transition in 2018) and I was immediately captivated. In addition to being beautiful, she was smart, feisty and very much a woman comfortable in her own skin. A professional dancer who put her career on hold for her man, a model for several of his album covers and an accomplished entrepreneur in her own right, Frances Davis continues to march to the beat of her own drum with style, verve and humor. There's not a lot about clothes, but Frances is such a great conversationalist that I believe you'll enjoy our chat.*

I read that when you first met Miles Davis, that you were unimpressed. Is that true?

I was performing with the Kathrine Dunham Company at Ciro's on the

Sunset Strip. We were a hit. A lot of celebrities were coming there to see us, including Sammy Davis, Jr., Roy Calhoun, Hugh O'Brien, Tom Hornell of Hornell meats, I mean it was heavyweight. When Max Roach, Miles's friend, came out to see the show, he told Miles that 'there's a little girl in that Katherine Dunham company who can dance her ass off'. So, Miles comes out to see who this is. And of course, he was smitten like all the rest of the men. He was one of many (laughs)!

At that time, I was too into my craft to respond to any of them. I didn't really know that much about his music. I knew about Johnny Mathis. When he saw me, of course he was taken aback! He wrote his name on a piece of paper and his telephone number and left it at the hotel next door. And I did call him, and we did go out a couple of times. I'm impressed a little when I found out who he was, but nothing huge. I went back to Chicago to see my family before I went to Europe and he had a gig in Chicago. He had dinner at my family's home, and he asked for my hand in marriage then! My father said 'no' and I'm saying 'no. How did this happen?'

What was it that changed your mind and how did you come around?

Much later, when I was with the Dunham Company, there was a singer/dancer from Haiti, and he joined the company. We ended up getting married and had a son with him, Jean-Pierre. But as I found out in this life, anybody I get involved with, they're always jealous. I had to call my father to come and get me and my son and take me back to Chicago, because I couldn't handle the jealousy. And in Chicago, I get a call for me to come into New York to do 'Porgy and Bess' at City Center. My family agreed to take care of my little boy while I went off to New York.

('Porgy and Bess') was closing, 'Mr. Wonderful', with Sammy Davis, Jr., was on Broadway at the time. I went to him and said 'Porgy and Bess' is closing, can I come over? He said 'of course'. To make a long story short, I'm going to rehearsal and Miles is coming down the street, 52nd and Broadway, and he looks at me and says, 'now that I have found you', I'll never let you go. And I didn't leave him until I left running for my life, nine years later.

You're known as a woman of style and taste. Was it vice versa or did

you both influence each other?

It was probably both. I always had my style and Miles had his style. I used to go with Miles to his Italian tailor, Mario. Italian chic. I used to get my clothes at Jax, which was THE place, a lot of ladies in the business, including Marilyn Monroe, bought her clothes there. When Miles found out I was buying my clothes there, he would buy me clothes there, especially when he was bad. Those clothes were very sexy, short. He'd buy them for me, then he'd say, 'where you going in that?' I had great legs. When I became a short-order cook when he wouldn't let me perform anymore, I would do the cooking in the kitchen in little short dresses in high heels.

Some of the things he did was outrageous, so I told my manager friend at Jax, 'ok send him to David Webb'. That was THE jeweler in New York, enough with the dresses! It wasn't easy being married to the genius, but we were so chic, both of us when we'd get in the Ferrari, that sleek Ferrari, the way he dressed, the way I dressed, we were something to behold.

What was he like when it came to clothes?

He knew what he wanted. He would explain to the tailor, and the tailor would do exactly what he wanted. We didn't go out that much, but I remember we went to an opening night and I picked his clothes that night. I was picking his clothes so much that when we got to the theater something was wrong, I ended up having my shoes on the wrong feet. He had to have his stuff done first, but it's ok, that's the way it was.

Which of his outfits did you love seeing him wear?

Well, I loved his suits. The way they fit! They were sensational looking.

How would he dress when you guys were around the house?

Normal, nothing outstanding. I was the outstanding one, with the short skirts. He was loose, laid back. I was always dressed, even when I went to the market. Since a little girl, I was always a dresser.

Miles would do crazy things; he would call in the middle of the afternoon and say 'I wanna have my manager over here. I want to have a turkey dinner.' In the middle of the afternoon! That means I had to go get the turkey...to tell you everything I went through with Miles Davis...

It sounds like it was an adventure, was it?

Anybody else would have been under the sanitarium. But I had a lot of love, and I knew who I was, no matter what he did to me. I was in the original West Side Story and opening night I received the Gypsy Robe for outstanding dancer. About eight months later, he came to the theater, picked me up in his Ferrari and said, 'A woman should be with her man. I want you out of West Side Story'. I froze. What do you do? I was naïve and sweet, a Libra, and I got out.

I don't know much about Libras, what does that mean?

We're love children, but we have a problem with balancing. But we're such givers. And I am loved by a lot of people. When I did leave 'West Side', Miles and I were at the Copacabana. Lena Horne was performing and Jerome Robbins, he's the one who choreographed 'West Side Story'. He come over to our table and said to Miles, 'can she at least do the movie (of 'West Side Story')?' Miles said, 'I'll let you know later'. He said to me later, 'is that MF kidding? Does he think I'm going to let you do the movie?' So, I couldn't do the movie.

Sammy Davis called and wanted me to join the cast of 'Golden Boy' as the ingénue. Miles had to be in Philadelphia for a gig, so I went to rehearsal to see how I could be involved. The next morning, we were on the Philadelphia Turnpike, going back to New York. That was the answer, so I couldn't do it.

Why do you think more than 20 years since he passed, why do you think he's a style icon?

When I left, he started wearing some weird looking clothes, to me. His hair was kind of wild. Everybody said when it came to me and my clothes, that he really wanted to be me. So maybe he let that all out after I left. Sometimes he looked like he could've been wearing makeup or something. Totally different from the chic Miles that I was with.

Your time together as a couple is the most talked-about era focused

on when people talk about his unique style at its peak. Why do you think that is so?

He had it going. When he performed, that look was it. And his body, he worked out. I used to go with him up to Sugar Ray Robinson's gym. If he had not been a musician, he would have been a boxer. We had the whole set up in our basement, and believe me, I watched. And when it was needed, I definitely knew how to duck.

How would you describe Miles Davis in one word?

Give me a break, Michael. He couldn't handle it; he just couldn't handle it! The bottom line is I stayed with him because I loved him. When I couldn't take it anymore, I ran.

I've known **Quincy Jones** *for nearly thirty years. When I reached out to interview him about his memories of Miles Davis, he enthusiastically agreed.*

In his autobiography, Miles cited Quincy as one of his very best friends. For 'Q', the feeling was clearly mutual. In his excitement to talk about his 'brother from another mother', Quincy went into his archive and pulled out one of his shirts that Miles took from him so that he could paint on it. The painting on the back is of a woman standing with her legs spread, beneath a caption that reads, 'kiss me'. On the front of the shirt, Miles painted, 'Q- love Miles'.

When sitting down with the man who has won more Grammy Awards than anyone else (27), along with 79 nominations, Emmy Awards, Oscar nominations, countless film scores, endless charitable work and a tribe full of children (7), the conversation can tend to go all over the place. While I was there to talk about Miles, Quincy's history is so rich, and he's such a great storyteller, I'm confident you'll enjoy the tapestry of the conversation. Think of it as a jazz styled conversation.

A spry 80 years old at the time of this conversation, Quincy was busier than ever, but he took the time to reminisce about one of his dearest friends.

I started by showing him one of the photos that was under consideration for the cover of this book, taken by William Claxton.

I knew him. He was the second-best jazz photographer next to Herman Leonard. Miles knew how to play. He was an actor too.

An actor, How so?

Shit yeah. He and Sinatra remind me so much of each other. Real good friends, but more bark than bite. They both shared one phrase with me when I was young: 'how you like your eggs, motherfucker?' I had pleurisy and I was at the Chateau Marmont, so Miles called and said, 'how you like your eggs, motherfucker?' And Sinatra, no connection at all, I was at Warner Bros, doing my first album for him and I was locked in Dean Martin's room for the weekend and Frank, in his military uniform said 'Q, how do you like your eggs?' The same phrase, but it was with love.

I've heard a lot about Miles being tough on the outside but really tender on the inside. What do you think that was about?

Game. When I first met him, in 1951, we'd just recorded 'Kingfish', one of my first arrangements for Lionel Hampton. I was at the Blue Note, listening to Mingus and Billy Taylor, when I heard a voice behind me, 'yeah I was freakin' out with a few of my bitches the other night and I heard some little young motherfucker with Lionel Hampton trying to play like me.' He was trying to scare me, you know. And he did! It's a helluva first way to meet. I heard the voice behind me, and I recognized it immediately.

But the good news is, in Quincy Troupe's book ('Miles: The Autobiography), and I always read books backwards, Miles said I was one of his five best friends.

(Quincy then segues into his thoughts on the style of Jazz musicians back in the day)

See, that was part of the shit back then, 52nd street and the jazz mentality. 'Cause they dressed their asses off.

(Quincy then shows me a photo of himself from the forties from his book, 'The Complete Quincy Jones')

This is how we dressed in the forties, '45 or '46, the year before I met Ray Charles. This band did everything. We danced, we sang, we played against Cab Calloway, played with Lady Day.

(In the photo, Quincy points out a couple of items protruding from his suit jacket.

'Underwear. And that's sweet wine.')

Was Miles sharp, even back then?

Yeah, everybody was. Not Bird, 'cause the junkies didn't stay too sharp. And (Thelonious) Monk didn't know how to dress.

When you first met Miles, did you hit it off immediately as friends?

No. We didn't have time. I was little, 18 and travelling on the road with Lionel Hampton. 'Hamp' was bigger than Duke, Basie and Louie Armstrong. I learned so much. He wanted me in the band at 15. I wanted to be a gangster until I was 11.

When did you start carving out a relationship?

Gradually. We'd see each other on the road. I'd see him in Europe a lot. We just gradually eased into it, because I had nothing but respect for him. He was trying to find himself musically, because he wasn't one of the primo guys in the beginning. When friendships start, you don't make friends, you discover friends.

Did anyone else's style stand out to you at that time?

All of 'em! Are you kidding me?! Malcolm X...he used to sell dope in front of the Majestic Hotel. We used to travel 700 miles a night. That was union regulations, you couldn't exceed that. We'd get to Detroit, and Hamp had a lot of musicians. The Holy Rollers were on one side, the weed smokers behind them, that's where we were, and then the boozers and the junkies, and lived accordingly (laughs).

Was Montreux the first time you played together?

No. He was on 'Back on the Block'. It was Dizzy (Gillespie)'s last album, Ella (Fitzgerald)'s last album and Miles was on it too. It's historical and those were all of my idols. We had Pee Wee Marquette. He was a funny little motherfucker. He was a midget. We used to call him a half a motherfucker.

But those cats could dress, always. Max (Roach), Ray Brown, Nat Cole.

(We segue to Clark Terry, both Miles's and Q's trumpet teacher, then we switch gears when Quincy voices his disappointment over today's musicians and their lack of knowledge of music history).

Miles tried to get him (Clark) to teach him how to play. He was a big influence on Miles. Clark's story is that he was trying to get some pussy and Miles was bothering him. He said, 'leave me alone'. He didn't want to do that again when he met me when I was 12. He showed me how to get my embouchure right.

I talked to him yesterday. He's in Arkansas teaching. I just did an album with him and Snoop Dog. Him doing the mumbles and Snoop Dog doing the rap. The problem is, Americans don't know the history of their own music. I asked very respectable guys that I love: 'in your mind, what year was the origin of rap?' They all said about '71. And they associated it with the Black Panthers and Gil Scott Heron. They're so far off, man. We were rapping when I was five years old in 1939 in Chicago. Started with The Dirty Dozens! It started in 1929.

That's the problem I have with all of the kids. They wanna be rich, they wanna be famous, but they don't wanna work. Some fuckin' vodka and some wheels. And you know what? God walks out of the room when you're making music for money. We never made music for money or fame.

Never! Never! It was unheard of.

Aside from the music, what else would you say made Miles special?

Well, number one, he wanted to pretend that he came from the street. Miles is from a very wealthy family. But that was not cool to tell the guys back then. You had to come from the street. He found out very early that stylin' would work, and he played it to the hilt. It was not an accident. I think it was pretty organic. Part of his essence was to be different. But he had a business mind. He'd say, 'fuck it. You don't have to give me nothin', just give me a Ferrari.'

I know that young people are on your mind these days. What do you think they could learn from Miles?

It's not their fault. The school systems don't tell them what it is. They pull out all of the jazz and pop music and leave it for classical music. It's fucking insane. <u>Our</u> classical music is jazz and blues. It came from that, from Gospel, during slavery and the church music morphed into blues. At first it was about Jesus. Then, after 1865, it was about sex and bitches and whiskey. And we used to play those juke joints, because they were the only places Black people could go, for 100 years.

(Quincy mentioned earlier that he bought 25 copies of Miles' 'Kind of Blue' and gives them to young people. I ask him why)

Because that, to me, is one of the definitive jazz records. It has the evolution of bebop in it. I tell them, 'promise me you'll listen to this once a day'. The kids that have done it, I've seen them grow. Music is only 12 notes. All of the styles all over the world, from Bach, Beethoven, Basie, Bo Diddley, whatever, all 12 notes. Most of the time, they use eight. Most people can't hear 12 tone music.

It's the voice of God. You can't see it, you can't smell it, you can't taste it, can't touch it, but it's powerful shit, man.

What stands out the most for you with Miles, what did you love the most about him?

Let me put it like this: Nadia said to me, in my fifth year with her, 'Quincy, your music can never be more or less than you are as a human being'. That's what it's about. It's about who you are as a person. And every time you play, it's going to be something different. But he'd be talking some shit.

He was so fucking warm, man and loving. That's what I loved about him. He was just like Sinatra. Sinatra was bipolar. If he loved you, it was like a love you'd never experienced in your life. He left me that. (*shows me a gold signet ring on his pinky finger*). That's his family crest from Sicily.

In his autobiography, it's clear he had deep feelings for you.

Yeah, and he said (in the autobiography), 'Marlon Brando and Q don't know what I know, that they both tried to hit on Francis (Miles ex-wife) and gave her an engagement ring.' I said, 'Dewey, you know that's bullshit'. And he said, 'fuck it, it sounds good!' (laughs)

I've got to show you something. (*We walk over to a garment bag and Quincy removes a white silk shirt with a black banded collar*)

This motherfucker, in the middle of his 60th birthday, he gives me this (*shows me a black-shawl collared tuxedo jacket*) and fucks up my shirt. Motherfucker came over with my shirt and fucked it all up. He painted a chick with her legs open and it says, 'kiss me'. You know I could never get rid of that. He was something else, man.

How were you able to get him to do the show in Montreux in '91 even after he had sworn he was never going to do his old music again?

I know. He was talking shit. I told him, 'you owe it to Gil (Evans), man. Those collaborations you made with him; you can't let that down.' But you can't talk him into anything. He was upstairs with Flavor Flav, getting ready to do another hip-hop album, and he came downstairs, walked past his lawyer and everybody else, and started negotiating his own shit. He said to Claude (Nobbs, producer of the Montreux Jazz Festival), 'this shit's gonna be expensive, man.' I said, 'what do you mean expensive?' I said, 'Dewey (Miles' middle name), it's not a problem, the band's gonna work out perfectly.' He said, 'you don't understand, motherfucker, the shit's hard to play!'

So, in rehearsal he's still negotiating. We had Wallace Roney play all of his parts, because he didn't remember how it went. But we got to rehearsal and he said, 'I got it, motherfucker. Don't worry about it'. To be there conducting him, watching him in competition with his 25-year-old self at 65 was really beautiful. He died a few months later.

I loved that motherfucker, man.

What do you make of his appearance during the last few years of his life? He began to look pretty radical.

He understood the power of show business, like the rock and roll people do. He understood the drama. He was a drama monger. If it works, and people respond to it...

If you could describe him in one word, what would it be?

'Nano technology'. Because he was complex, man.

Bassist **Ron Carter** *is the most recorded bassist in history, having officially appeared on more than two thousand recordings. In addition to playing the double bass, Mr. Carter is also proficient on the cello. A multiple Grammy Award winner, Ron Carter is probably best known as the anchor for one of Miles Davis' greatest bands, a quintet consisting of Davis, Carter, Herbie Hancock, Wayne Shorter and Tony Williams. Still active today, Mr. Carter took a few minutes to talk about his storied history with Miles Davis.*

How did you and Miles meet?

He was doing a concert in Rochester New York in 1958. They were supposed to have him picked up at the concert by someone who was going to take him to the train station to continue on his tour to New York City. Whoever was supposed to pick him up never showed up, and knowing Paul Chambers, I was asked to give Miles and the band a ride to the train station in my car, which I did.

In 1963, you started working with Miles. What was the experience like for you?

Well, I was the bass player in the band, so I kinda had my way with him, so to speak. It was a wonderful time, it was a great relationship.

Not many people had their way with Miles, as I understand it. How did you easily get along with him?

I was the only bass player in the band, so I had a head start on everybody else. When he was looking for a replacement for Paul, who was leaving to join Wynton Kelly, I was working at the Half Note with Jim Hall and Art Farmer. He came by the club that night to see if I was interested in joining his band. I explained to him that I was working with Art Farmer for the next two weeks and if Art Farmer thought that he could do without me for the next two weeks, I'd be happy to go. If not, I was bound to finish my gig with Art Farmer.

So, he waited around, and Art agreed to let me go to join Miles and that kind of set the table for our relationship.

What would you say made the musical relationship special?

I don't know how to answer that question, man. We're two people in the laboratory together. We had our own experiments to work out, hopefully they wouldn't blow up.

What do you remember about Miles' dress sense and his style of clothing when you played with him?

Well, he had to get his clothes made. When he was working out at the gym, he was getting more muscular than off the rack suits would tolerate, I think. Wanting to look like just Miles, he found designers who could design clothes for him, as he felt he wanted to look like. That's only my guess.

When I joined the band, he had us go to this place on 48th street, around Rockefeller Center and had the guy who owned the place, Jack Reitbart, fit us with tuxedos and matching jackets and slacks, so he had the band tuned into his style of clothes right away.

How did that fit with your personal style?

I had my clothes made, since I was 6'4" and 170 pounds, it wasn't easy to find those sizes on the rack, so I was not unaccustomed to having stuff made just for me, in a general sense. My wardrobe wasn't as big as his, because I wasn't earning that kind of money and I wasn't as concerned about style as I was about fit. I kind of got to that zone later on in my career.

Was there any outfit he wore that stuck to your mind to this day?

He looked good in whatever he put on. That was the great thing about having stuff made for you that you liked. You could always wear it and feel comfortable.

What do you think his clothes said about him as a musician, and as a person?

That he had a sense of how he wanted to look. That it was HIS sense and not how everybody thought he should look.

Did he ever give you any fashion suggestions or did he leave you to your own devices?

We were left to our own devices. I was probably the one who best mirrored a personal style in dressing. I was kind of left to my own devices in general. I was checking the train schedule, making reservations for everybody. I was kind of in charge along that line and when you have that level of responsibility, I would like to think that he felt that anyone who knew how to do these things had a pretty good sense of how to look doing it.

Did he influence your style, or would you say it was vice versa?

Not really. He had his way. He had his look. Being eight or nine years older, he already found a look that was comfortable for him. I hadn't found that specific kind of look until I was able to earn a sufficient amount of money to be able to afford the kind of look that I thought I'd be able to look good in. I've maintained that dressing posture as we speak. It was important for him to look the part of the bandleader and he defined that look by the way he dressed.

I got an endorsement in Japan a couple of years ago by a company that makes men's suits, so they've got me into a really specific fit for me and my height. Standing up all night playing the bass, I need something that will tolerate that kind of liberal posture all night. The fit was a great fit. I'm in a strange physical position all night, and if I'm not careful, the suit's going to tear or have some strange weaves because I'm bent over all night. They found a way to make some clothes that makes my posture not interfere with the look of my clothes.

How would you describe your personal style?

Elegantly conservative (chuckles).

Why do you think Miles Davis is considered even to this present day as a style icon?

He was an important figure musically and people who are generally that important have a head in start in other areas of their life, according to a public's view of them. And it's because he was who he was and he had this magic about him that made him even more visible and more in a position to attract that kind of attention to what he wore because he was an important figure in the arts and it made him more of an interesting and curious item for people who wanted to know. This guy plays like that, no one he looks like that.

When was the last time you saw him?

It was about four years before he passed away. He used to live in my neighborhood. I'd kind of see him in the street, or I'd go by his house when he wasn't feeling well. He'd ask me to go to the Cuban restaurant in the neighborhood and pick him up something to eat. At that time, he was kind of immobile, with his hip issues and all that other stuff. Once he started travelling again, our paths didn't cross often.

How would you describe Miles Davis in a single word?

(Long pause) 'Interesting'.

4. SORCERER: 1967-1975

'You expect the unexpected from Miles Davis'

-Clive Davis

There are not enough of books, essays, poems and documentaries that give a detailed account of the volcanic era of the sixties. Whether one focuses on the unfortunate assassinations of popular American leaders, the country wide divide caused by the Vietnam war, free love, rock and roll or the ascendency of the civil rights movement, the sixties was a period that suggested endless possibilities, both good and bad. The broad strokes of change also trickled down to personal journeys, and those with adventure in their veins fully embraced the challenge. For someone like Miles Davis, this was nothing new; chaos was where he lived.

Creatively Miles was reaching for the stars again with his all-star quintet delivering the muscular, energetic *Miles Smiles*, the peculiar *Sorcerer* and the idiosyncratic *Nefertiti*. While all three albums have their moments, on reflection, it's clear that something new was in its embryonic stage, even though the mad scientist toiling away in in the lab didn't quite yet know what it was.

Miles kept pushing, changing musicians as often as was needed, and edging ever closer to the new sound he was trying to capture. He gained focus with help from Gil Evans on one of the first fusion albums, *Filles de Kilimanjaro*. A blend of jazz ideas tweaked by electric instruments and rock foundation, a possible clue that helped shape Miles new vision found in the title of one of the tracks, *Mademoiselle Mabry*, dedicated to his soon to be second wife, the twenty-three year-old model, singer and songwriter, Betty Mabry, who was also featured on the album's cover.

Their relationship and subsequent marriage was short-lived, but Betty's influence on Miles had long-lasting effects, resulting in a change from Italian suits to snakeskin clothes, and musically from 'Trane, Diz and Max to Hendrix, Sly and Cream. Betty had great taste. She was the toast of the hippest New York scene and was as crazy about Miles as he was about her. Her youth and beauty probably didn't hurt either.

Betty came along at the right time. Miles had grown frustrated watching artists like Cannonball Adderley find favor with an R&B audience while sax player Charles Lloyd was welcomed into the rock world. Miles felt like a man without a country. While he wasn't one to try and fit in, he also wasn't welcome to the idea of being irrelevant. Having always been on the cutting edge of everything, Miles realized a kindred spirit in Betty and was surprisingly open to the fashion and funk that she exposed him to.

Betty Davis introduced him to the music of the day. Rock and funk was her thing and Miles saw value in it musically and also as an opportunity to expand his audience. Current funk and R&B revitalized him as a longtime creative force. Miles couldn't sit by and watch music pass him by, especially when Betty's influence connected with him in such a profound way, it was impossible.

As he explored who he was and how he fit into the cultural landscape, his clothes began to mirror his evolution. Betty Davis is generally credited with changing his look from European finery to funky fly threads, but according to Ms. Davis herself, she didn't have as much to do with the change in Miles' look as many would think. "He just got tired of wearing suits", she said. As has been cited over and over, Miles had a great eye and knew what looked good on him. Always conscious of his image, Miles was undoubtedly aware of the contradiction of introducing his audiences to a brand-new sound, while still holding on to his old look that to him, at least, was outdated.

During his fashion exploration, Miles sometimes went from looking like a funky spaceman to an action hero from the then-popular Blaxploitation movie craze. But given his already iconic status, no matter how 'out there' he might have looked, he wore it with confidence and more swagger, which as people agreed, he pulled off the looks more than anyone else could. As noted in his autobiography, he acknowledged that the casualness of rock bands and audiences might have impacted his exploration into a new style of dress. In addition to dashikis and robes, Miles began wearing Indian tops created by an Argentinian designer named Hernando, who had a shop in the Village. He got suede pants from Steven Burrows, a black designer and had shoes made in London from a shop called Chelsea Cobblers.

Betty took him to some of her favorite shops in the Village and Miles began amassing his collection of exotic skins: leather shirts, snakeskin and suede pants, while buying a lot of brightly colored silk shirts in huge quantities, that he never wore more than one time.

Musically Miles continued tinkering. He brought in young but immensely talented guitarist George Benson to replace Joe Beck, looking for more funk from the sound. Referencing James Brown, Miles began to let the rhythm section set the tone and dominate, instead of the soloist being the main focus of the music. The lessons of Sly and James Brown were beginning to take root in Miles' unique point of view.

The changes continued with more new players. Chick Corea and David Holland replaced Herbie Hancock and Ron Carter on keys and bass, respectively. During this period, guitarist John McLaughlin and saxophonist Wayne Shorter also joined the band for varying periods.

This new style resulted in longer songs as Miles continued to look at other new music trends, like Indian music. The seeming simplicity of that style brought forth more focused attention on fewer chords, a concept that was adopted by disciples of psychedelic music and others, most notably The Beatles.

Miles realized that his new approach gave him room to roam with his instrument, coming in wherever he felt appropriate, while still working within a structured style.

He started focusing on playing in venues that generally featured rock acts, moving away from more traditional jazz clubs. He played on bills with Santana, Grateful Dead, Laura Nyro and Steve Miller Band. Clive Davis, who was running Columbia, was supportive of Miles' new direction and encouraged him to play venues like the Filmore East.

1970 showcased Miles' most direct attempt to cultivate his new audience, with the two-disc release of *Bitches Brew*. He continued to experiment with the alchemy of his band, adding more power to his rhythm section by featuring three more drummers along with Holland- Lenny White, Jack De Johnette and Don Alias. He rounded the band up with the bass of Harvey Brooks and bass clarinet by Been Maupin. He broke his long-standing rule of only musicians in the studio and had Betty at his side, looking for her critical feedback.

Rock journalists loved the record, captivated by the long, expansive tunes that included compositions by Wayne Shorter and John McLaughlin, but the rock audience was confused and reacted to the record with nonchalance. In the rock world, trumpet barely existed, let alone as the focal point of a band. Miles, as being who he was didn't give up, rather he kept introducing the rock audience to his unique style by playing in front of larger crowds than he'd ever experienced before, possibly peaking at the Isle of Wight Pop Festival in 1970 to nearly a half million people.

Bursting with new ideas, Miles continued to spend time in the studio with young, creatively open musicians and stayed focused on forging new musical directions. When the soundtrack to *Jack Johnson* was offered to him, Miles said 'yes' immediately. Being a fan of the late heavyweight champion and a life-long boxer himself, the soundtrack allowed Miles to express himself musically with power, aggression and a groove, ably supported by new bassist, 19-year old Michael Henderson, just coming off of successful sessions and tours with Marvin Gaye, Stevie Wonder and Aretha Franklin. All-star drummer Billy Cobham brought his strength and steady beat to bear, anchoring grooves that could run 20 minutes or more.

As his music got bolder and more abstract, so did his wardrobe. Furs, leathers, wrap-around glasses were par for the course. His flamboyant wardrobe reflected the sometimes outlandish, hard to fathom music, but also reinforced that Miles Davis didn't follow trends, he was a trendsetter, and it didn't matter whether anyone followed him or not.

His final studio album of the era (live albums and unreleased compilations made up the balance of his output for the rest of the decade), *On the Corner*, was Miles' most blatant attempt to court the contemporary R&B audience. They weren't having it, neither were the critics. Critics derided Miles more for *On the Corner* than probably any other album he recorded. Young Black kids just ignored it, ironically preferring the funk of The Ohio Players, The Isley Brothers, James Brown and other R&B acts who influenced Miles.

During this period, he split with Betty after a year of marriage; it's been said that she was too wild for him, but his bad habits certainly didn't help, nor did his affair with Marguerite Eskridge, who would bear him his last child, and son, Erin. Reckless adventures like being shot at, concern about upset drug dealers and Mafioso threats didn't help him keep a relationship either. Miles' bad habits began to catch up with him.

Alcohol and cocaine were commonplace, arrests for drug possession, bleeding ulcers and nodes on his throat suddenly became Miles' reality. His health started to deteriorate at a swift rate, resulting in an operation for his hip joints. And as if that wasn't enough, he broke both ankles when he fell asleep in his car while speeding down the West Side Highway and totaled his lime green Lamborghini. Another version of the story says he was trying to cross three lanes to make the 125th street exit and so he hit the stone exit ramp, but however it went down, so did Miles.

In addition to his troubles, Miles had a lot of death to mourn and grieve. The deaths of his parents in the early-mid sixties still haunted him. The sudden deaths of Jimi Hendrix, Duke Ellington, Paul Chambers, Wynton Kelly and probably the most painful loss of all, John Coltrane who died from liver cancer at the young age of 40 all hit him hard.

In the summer of '75, Miles hit a wall: suffering from poor health, exhaustion, depression and self-abuse from substances internal and external, he went into his Manhattan brownstone, closed the door and didn't come out for almost five years.

Sorcerer

CONVOS

Andrea Aranow is a fashion legend. In addition to creating memorable clothes for Miles Davis and Jimi Hendrix, she was a designer for Alexander McQueen and has pioneered the art of textile collecting, amassing more than 26,000 pieces in her collection from around the world. Long regarded as one of the foremost experts on vintage textiles, Andrea's collection has been featured in a number of prolific exhibits and she continues to grow her archive!

Before we get to Miles, I have to ask: What was it like to make clothes for Jimi Hendrix?

Jimi was a different story! He was so shy he wouldn't talk to me directly. He came in the first time and he didn't speak to me. He had these girls with him, and he'd tell the girls and the girls would tell me. I made quite a few clothes for Jimi and eventually he started talking, but not much, compared with Miles. He was always pushing the limits. He was always encouraging me to push out a little farther. He was a good client.

How did you meet Miles Davis?

I had a very hip store in the East Village on East 9th Street. A few music people were coming in and I was getting a lot of press from my first snakeskin suit for Jimi Hendrix and it just kept going, in that crazy, spiral kind of way that things did in those days. Miles came in and he brought in (then wife) Betty and then he brought in his (then) current partner, Marguerite, who I'm still friendly with.

How did he find out about you?

I don't remember who brought him in, but we were just a block or two from the Filmore East and it was a little street of boutiques and people trying out their crazy ideas. He loved to preen, so it was natural. And I loved to make clothes for people who wanted to be seen. I was pretty shy about wearing that stuff myself, but I liked dressing other people, so it was a pretty good match.

What was your experience styling Miles?

Well, the years that I knew him, he was pretty erratic. Temperamentally with his clothes and everything else, but he really appreciated his clothes and liked to dress his ladies and liked to dress himself. I made him some clothes, and then some clothes for the women, and I visited his house on 77th or 79th. I was really overwhelmed when he invited me to take a look in his bedroom and his wall long closet. I was just in my early twenties then, so the life of the rich and famous was quite big.

Why do you think it was overwhelming?

It was probably a thirty-foot closet filled with finery. It was a time when a lot of styles were being explored at once, like Edwardian Dandy. Miles was pretty much in that Dandy thing, as far as clothes I made for him. Not necessarily for the shapes but dressing up with accessories. He was never looking for the Marlboro Man type of aesthetic.

When you started working with him, how did you figure out what worked?

I think Miles came in with his own ideas, but pretty quickly encouraged me to suggest what I thought was good for him and followed my lead.

What was it about Miles that inspired your creativity? What did you think would look great on him?

I was working quite a bit with cobra skin, which had a very slick surface, flat and slick. So, I played off of that. It's a kind of difficult material, it doesn't drape. We had to do all of the fittings in muslin that had to be very specifically tailored. I kind of played off of the 'gloss' of him, you know? I thought of Miles as being somebody who would work well with shines and flames and that kind of stuff. He was a lot more articulate than many of my customers, that's for sure.

In terms of knowing what he liked?

Knowing what he liked, and just expressing himself well with a vocabulary and imagery that was communicative...but other times he wouldn't talk much. When he wanted to talk, he could express himself very well verbally.

You said earlier that he was erratic. How so?

He was moody. I think he was using pretty much, so his mood was swinging all over the place.

Did he style Betty, or did she come in with her own ideas?

He was still married to Betty, but he was already seeing Marguerite (Cantu), so I can't say if he got Betty that cape to appease her. I don't know how it went.

Was there any one particular piece that you created for him that stands out to you?

I don't have pictures of any of those clothes, unfortunately. It was a bit of a blur. Sorry to disappoint you on that.

You were working with Miles in the early seventies?

Yeah. Erin (Miles' son by Marguerite) was born in '71. I hung out a lot with Marguerite because we were both pregnant at the same time. Both our sons were born within a couple of months of each other. I probably started working with him in '68 or '69. I didn't keep my business going for too long; I closed it in '73. With Miles, it was the late '60s, early '70s.

One of the consistent contradictions in my research is Miles' height. It ranges from 5'4" to 5'9". Do you have any idea?

I'd say he was closer to 5'8", he certainly wasn't 5'4. He was fairly slight when I knew him. Pretty much on the skinny side from previous photos that I'd seen, but his height wasn't changing.

If you could describe Miles in one word, what would it be?

'Curious'. He got into a lot of stuff beyond fashion and music. (Pause) But I have to tell you, I don't think I knew him at his best. He was already having some problems when I knew him. I loved his music, and I loved working with him, but when he walked in the door, I was never exactly sure who was coming in. His moods changed quite a bit.

I spent an afternoon at his house. That was kind of good, because we got to hang out for a few hours, and he was more relaxed than usual. The guy was in a hurry most of the time. But there we were just hanging out and I got to see his closet. I'd never seen a round bed before! Marguerite was there, trying on clothes that I had just finished. We were taking pictures...it was a good afternoon. He had Egyptian symbols painted on the walls in his back garden. He clearly was not limited in his reach.

Perhaps the most important element in the perception of Miles Davis's fashion icon status besides the man himself is a vast number of photographs that have been taken of him over the years. From the fifties through the end of his life, Miles Davis has been featured in thousands of photos, many of which are nearly as iconic as some of his most beloved albums. One of those photographers who became a good friend of the musician is **Anthony Barbosa**. *Also well regarded as a writer, historian and artist, Barbosa is still an active artist with exhibits featured in prestigious museums and galleries around the world. For a look at a selection of his body of work, visit barbosastudio.com*

How did you meet Miles?

I was hired by Essence magazine in 1971, and it was about his clothes! That's why I took the photograph in front of the closet with the all the

clothes. And then I had some other shots of him.

What was he like?

Oh, I was scared shitless, because everybody said he was evil! But as it turned out, we were friends for twenty years. He was wonderful. We got along really well. He forced Columbia Records to let me do an album cover (*You're Under Arrest*) of him, and it was just me and him and the ideas we came up with. Nobody else could come from the

record company. He was really nice to me. I photographed him a number of times.

He had all those clothes in the closet in 1971. He told me he would go and buy expensive shirts, but after the concert was over, they were so sweaty, he'd throw them away. So, you never saw him in the same shirt. And he wasn't spending $20 on his shirts.

When you shot him for the first time, did you need any help from a stylist?

No. There was no stylist. He just got different clothes that he had at that time and put 'em on. I did everything in his apartment. There are a

111

number of other shots, but everybody seemed to like the ones of him in front of the closet. There are other ones as well.

Is there any one photo that says to you, 'that's Miles'.

I did a story for the New York Times magazine, and it's also in the New York Times book. It's a portrait of him. That's Miles. It was considered by Life magazine one of the photos of the year, years ago. That really exemplifies him, the look on his face. But the one black & white, of him next to his closet, everybody seems to want to buy that photo, so I don't know…

I had a contact from Japan one year, they were afraid to approach Miles to do a TV commercial. I told Miles about it, and they agreed to let me co-direct the TV commercial. They were doing it for a liquor. They bought some clothes by Issey Miyake. When he saw the clothes, he didn't want to wear Miyake's clothes. He went out, the night before the shoot and spent seven thousand dollars on clothes that he bought himself. He agreed to wear one of Issey Miyake's tops. But I shot him in his own clothes as well. He had some nice jackets, a red jacket and a gold jacket. He liked to pick out his own clothes.

Prior to that had you directed a commercial before?

No! They wanted me, because he could be rough. So, they let me direct him. I got half of the crew and they brought some of the crew. The guy from Japan directed the cameraman, I directed Miles via storyboard. He was wonderful. He did whatever I said. He was always good to me. He knew mainly musicians, see. And I wasn't a musician, so we could talk about other things. He was great.

You said some time ago, and I quote, 'when I do a portrait, I'm doing a photograph of how that person feels to me, how I feel about the person, not how the person looks. In order for the portraits to work, I have to make a mental connection as well as an emotional one'. Can you talk about that as it regards Miles?

Miles was always on guard. He was very intelligent. He could sense certain things about people. But because he knew me, he would do whatever I asked to do. At times, he was like a little boy, sort of shy. There's another side of Miles that people don't know.

He was like that from the beginning. Somebody had sent a white photographer to shoot him (this was way before me) and he that photographer wait downstairs for four hours before he even came down. The hairdresser knew me, named Finney. Finney must have said some nice things about me, and I ended up spending the whole day there. He had a two-thousand-page French cookbook. He made French soup that was unbelievable.

I think it was, for a change, he saw a Black photographer come to his house. And I don't know what I did in those years. I'm not a pushy kind of guy. It was a shock to me because everybody else said he could be tough. He was never that for me. I used to stretch canvases for him when he started painting because I knew how to do it.

He liked some hat I was wearing once that I bought in the Village and he had me buy different colors for him.

How would you describe his style back then when you were first getting to know him?

Oh, he had all kinds of clothes. He just stood out. He just followed his own feelings. He might have been one way in the forties, and he dressed the way he was, as a person. In the fifties, he might have been another way, I didn't know him then. In the seventies, he dressed just as he was, as a person. 'This is me'. But there's more than one 'me' in him. He's a Gemini, there's more than one personality there. The way you see him is the way you think he is, but to other people, he's a different way. He's a very complex person, a very complex person.

One time I was in Malibu and he went for a swim. He used to swim every morning, about a mile. He came out and he had all of these rubber bands in his hair and he asked me to take them out, but his hair was wet, and we had to go to Watts to get them out. That was the first time I'd ever seen him humbled. The barber said, 'what the fuck did you do to your hair, Miles?' He was like a little boy.

Why in your opinion do you think he had the rubber bands in his hair?

I don't know why, but I couldn't take them out.

Can you tell me about the *You're Under Arrest* session?

He called me and said 'Tony I want you to do my next album cover and it's called *You're Under Arrest*. After he hung up, the art director from Columbia Records called me and said, 'Miles won't let me come to the shoot!' I said, 'you never hired me to do any shoots, so what do I care?' So, I told Miles that he called. He said 'that motherfucker, every time we do a shoot, he uses some of the money and buys drugs', and so he didn't want him on the shoot. So, it was just me and Miles on the shoot. I had gotten a toy machine gun and he brought a lot of different clothes. I decided I would make the background blood red. I shot him in the different jackets that he had.

The one that they finally used was not my favorite, because I wanted him to be more sinister, there's another shot that I like more because he's looking at you at a glance. They picked one where he's looking straight ahead. They had nothing to do with the concept. We spent the day doing it.

The day I heard he passed, I cried. We were close in so many ways.

"I'd never seen anybody like her. When she showed up, Oh My God! ... She came down out of a cloud to save all mankind!" That's Miles Davis bassist Michael Henderson dreamily describing the first time he saw Miles' second wife, **Betty Davis**. *Generally credited with opening Miles Davis up to new music and fashion in the early seventies, Betty Davis had carved a niche for herself as a unique fashion model, a style icon, a muse for both Davis and good friend Jimi Hendrix, as well as a pioneer of sexually aggressive and musically challenging funk- rock. In my conversation with Ms. Davis, it was difficult to reconcile the humble and almost shy voice on the phone as the woman who has been described more than once as 'the original Madonna.'*

How did you develop your interest in fashion and your unique point of view, growing up in Pittsburgh?

I went to the Fashion Institute of Technology in New York, and I majored

in apparel design. After I quit school, I started modeling, and being exposed to the fashion world helped give me my sense of style. Stephen Burrows, a designer, was a good friend of mine and used to design clothes for me. I modeled for all of the top designers, like Halston, Scott Berry, Stephen Burrows and Norma Kamali.

You moved to New York when you were what, 16?

Yes. I graduated a year early from high school.

Did you have any fear of moving to a city that big?

No, I didn't have any fear. My father's sister lived there, and his relatives lived there. So, I wasn't going to a weird environment, it was actually a family-oriented environment.

How did the modeling career kick-off for you?

I went to several agencies, and Wilhelmina signed me.

Were you making music while you were modeling?

I was always doing the music. I always wrote music from the time I was twelve. My first song was 'Baking the Cake of Love'. I started developing my music, but when I got married, I stopped writing for a while. Miles told me that I was developing something else. That's when I got into arranging music.

What did he mean by you were 'developing something else'?

Well, I told him, 'Miles, I'm not writing anymore, and I'm really scared'. He said, 'don't worry about it; you're just developing something else'.

Why were you scared?

I was really into my music and I just got very nervous about not being able to write anymore. It's just like if you're a musician and you have an instrument and all of a sudden you can't play anymore; you just get scared.

Was it writer's block?

I don't know what it was, but he said I was developing something else, so I started restructuring my songs. I started writing bass lines and guitar lines and piano lines. So, it turned out that I was truly developing something else.

How did you and Miles meet?

I went to a dance concert, and I saw this great looking guy in this great looking suit, and I wondered who he was. At intermission, I thought I'd go up and introduce myself and tell him that I really liked his suit. I went into this big hall, but I couldn't find him, I didn't see him. The next day I called a photographer that I know, Guy Turrell, and said, 'Guy, I went to this dance concert last night and saw this guy and you might know him. He had this great suit on'. Guy said it sounded like Miles Davis. I didn't know who he was. I asked Guy 'who is Miles Davis?' He said 'come on Betty, you don't know who Miles Davis is? He's a great musician, he plays the trumpet, he plays jazz'. He told me that Miles usually played at the Village Gate and the Village Vanguard. I called the Village Gate and the Village Vanguard to find out when he was going to be appearing there. So, I went down to the Village Gate and looked at him while he was onstage, and I couldn't connect him with the guy at the dance concert, because he wasn't dressed the same.

How was he dressed?

I think he was just wearing a shirt and trousers. He wasn't wearing a suit. At intermission I went to make a phone call, and a guy came up and tapped me on the shoulder. It was Miles's trainer, Bobby. He used to train Miles at the gym. He said 'Miles Davis would like to know if you'd have a drink with him upstairs'. I said, 'sure, why not'. I went upstairs, we met each other. He had a great sense of humor. He said come over and sit on my hand. I laughed, he took me home and that's how I met him.

(At this point, John Ballon, who connected me with Betty and was on the call, prompted her to recall the very first time they met, when she tracked him down and showed up at his home.)

He opened the door and saw me, then asked 'what do you want?' I told him it was a long story, and he said, 'I don't have time for a long story', and then I left.

What was it about him that struck you so hard and drew you to him immediately?

It was the way he looked. He had a great nose, and he had a lot of style. I just really was attracted to him, that's all.

How would you describe his style when you met him?

He wore great suits. He used to have a tailor named Maria. Maria used to make all of his suits. I used to go with him when he'd have his fittings. He wore great shoes and he just looked great in clothes.

How tall was Miles? I can't seem to get a consensus.

He was about 5'8". I'm 5'7" and he was just a little bit taller than me.

How would you describe <u>your</u> style back then?

Since I was modeling for the designers, I would get some of their clothes, and I used to go to a lot of shops in New York like Hernando's,

Madonna's, De Noyers.

(John asked about a shop run by a woman named Colette who made clothes for Betty, Miles and Jimi Hendrix)

Her shop didn't have a name. Miles didn't really shop there. I shopped there. It was mostly for women's clothing. They would give Jimi shirts, but he didn't really shop there.

I spoke with Andrea Aranow who used to make snakeskin clothes for you and Miles?

Yeah, I used to wear Andrea's clothes. She made a snakeskin cape and things like that.

From what I read, you exposed him to different kinds of music and style. Was he open to it or resistant?

He was all for it. He just didn't want to wear suits anymore. I guess it was the times and he was interested in dressing differently. I liked him in the suits, I really did. But that was his taste at the time, and I had to go along with it.

Would you say you helped him figure out his new style?

I really didn't. He'd just come to the stores with me when I shopped. He shopped at the same stores that I did. It was just his taste at the time. The stores I went to were unisex, except for De Noyers, which was a man's store. I used to get slacks from there, leather pants from there.

His clothes and music seemed to have evolved around the same time. Was really the case or did one lead to the other?

The clothes were before the music.

Were you introducing him to new music or new artists?

He would listen to the music I'd play at the house. If he liked it, he would tell me.

What were you listening to?

Jimi Hendrix, Otis Redding, Sly Stone and James Brown. Miles was listening to a lot of classical: Rachmaninoff, Stravinsky, Mozart.

Was Miles particular about his clothes? Did he take care of them?

He was very self-conscious about the way he looked. He was very into the way he looked. He knew how he wanted to look before he got dressed. I didn't voice my opinion, because it was the way he wanted to look. Like he didn't voice his opinion about the way I wanted to look.

Was there a particular outfit that completely stood out that you thought he looked great in while you were together?

Just the suits. All of the suits, but they never came out when I was with him.

Do you remember the first thing he bought beyond the suits?

He got some suede pants from Hernando's and Hernando made him a matching jacket. He took to it right away. It was his choice.

Did he ever ask you for fashion suggestions, or did he just go with his gut all of the time?

I would pick out things like scarves, belts and shirts for him. But his jackets and trousers he'd pick out for himself. He started wearing clogs at the time, so he stopped wearing the Italian shoes.

If you could describe Miles Davis in one word, what would it be?

'Fantastic'. I'll tell you for example: I went into the post office and there's a stamp of Miles. I looked at that picture on the stamp and said 'that's the Miles I married'. Because there was nothing but lines, like architecture, the way he was standing, the way he was holding the trumpet…I was floored. If I didn't know him, I would have fallen in love all over again.

5. DARK MAGUS: 1975-1980

'His organism is tired. And after all the music he's contributed for thirty-five years, he needs a rest'. – Gil Evans on Miles Davis

Much has been written, rumored, speculated, fabricated and even mythologized about the self-imposed five-year retirement that Miles Davis entered during the last half of the seventies and the beginning of the eighties. As *MilesStyle* is focused on the sartorial excellence of Miles Davis, this period offers little to review or ponder when it comes to his dress and sense of fashion. But as a part of his legend, it warrants at least a brief acknowledgment.

Not many pictures are available from this period and of the ones that have surfaced, few are complimentary. One could argue that clothes and fashion found themselves at the bottom of his list of priorities during this period. When anything is written about how he looked while on 'sabbatical', he's either described as being dressed in all black with his large wraparound sunglasses (whether day or night), or rumpled and disheveled.

It seems the combination of bad health and a less than secure foothold in the popular music of the day pounced on Miles, and he just didn't have the energy to fight to get back up this time. In addition to the ailments listed in the previous chapter, add the following maladies:

Gallstones

Various complications brought on by sickle cell anemia

More hip surgery

Leg infection caused by injecting himself with a dirty needle

An infected leg that was nearly amputated

Rumors of throat cancer and radiation treatment

Then add copious amounts of narcotics, (with cocaine at the top of the heap) chased down with a lot of wine, not to mention volatile relationships with women that often turned violent, and we have a genius who was way too worn out to be inspired.

Stories abound about his violence, his tendency to hallucinate and his general lack of enthusiasm for anything during this period. Miles himself admitted to behavior unbecoming a man who on several occasions changed the face of music. In his controversial autobiography, Miles expresses regret for some of his behavior during the 'Dark Age', but rarely tries to defend his actions and accepts that it wasn't the best representation of himself.

Contrary to legend, Miles did try a half-hearted return to music. In 1978, he went into the studio, played the organ and never touched the trumpet. He was unhappy with the result and retreated from his first love for another year and a half.

Music during this period proved difficult for Miles. His various physical infirmities made playing his instrument too painful, which only added to his reticence to return. And the current music scene at the time didn't hold his interest. The realization that the audiences of the day weren't as enamored with his last few releases as they had been with his classic material didn't help get him out of the house.

In interviews about this period, Miles uses the word 'bored' often. Physically limited, unable to fall back on healthy crutches like boxing and swimming, musically uninspired by what he was listening to and what he thought audiences wanted from him, drugs and alcohol abuse probably helped ease some of the pain temporarily, but not enough to shake him out of his funk, which was to last for several years. But the story doesn't end here for the musician. Fortunately, *Miles Ahead*, the first film based on Miles Davis, centers on a fictitious story set in 1979, near the end of his longest, darkest night. To supplement a part of his life that allows for no clear consensus, what follows is an enlightening conversation with the film's Costume Designer Gersha Phillips, who had to fill in the blanks on how Miles might have dressed during this period.

MILESSTYLE

Dark Magus

CONVOS

He is eclectic, in both music and fashion, and clearly walks to the beat of his own drum. He is curious, restless, funky, jazzy, rocky, stylish and elegant. With each of those descriptions, one could be talking about Miles Davis, or one of rock music's most versatile artists, **Lenny Kravitz**. *The Grammy Award-winning singer/songwriter/actor has been on the music scene carving out a unique path for himself for over twenty-five years. Kravitz knew Miles Davis as a child and had a relationship with Davis that has left its mark on both his approach to work and life.*

In an interview with <u>Oceansidedrive.com</u> you describe (director, photographer) Gordon Parks thusly: 'That's beautiful that this guy can express himself in many different ways and not be inside a box.'" You could have been talking about Parks, Miles or yourself. Clearly not having limitations put on you is an important thing.

I see creativity as a way of life without limitations. For me living is an art that has no boundaries, which enables me to use different mediums to express myself. At a young age I opened myself through my experiences and therefore I could not relate to "the box".

You knew Miles initially as a friend of your parents. What was that like?

I found Miles to be dark and mysterious. Not dark in a negative way, but deep in tone and vibe. When he was in the room the mood changed.

When did you realize who he really was? Did that have any impact on you?

I finally understood who Miles was after my family moved from New York to Los Angeles and we used to go see him perform at the Playboy Jazz Festival at the Hollywood Bowl. That was when I got to know him as a performer and a musical force. The impact was monumental and forged an impression that is still with me to this day.

Did his path influence or impact way the direction of your career?

Miles' influence on me was all about me finding my creative freedom.

You are a product of a biracial marriage. You decided to become a musician with a variety of interests, with rock being one of them. You seem to wear your racial identity with relative grace. When you look at what Miles dealt with as a black man coming up against racism both subtly and sometimes physically, yet never reluctant to speak truth to power, how does that resonate to you?

I love that Miles had no filter vocally. From what I had witnessed, he always spoke his mind. I have personally seen Miles destroy someone that had it coming to them. It may not be my way but based on the racism he encountered in his time I can understand it. Sometimes the truth has to be delivered in a hardcore manner.

You mentioned in an interview with Elvis Mitchell on 'The Treatment', that you have a leather jacket that Miles gave you. What were the circumstances of that moment and could you describe the jacket?

I had just finished a leg of an American tour shortly after Miles died and I went by my Godmother Cicely (Tyson)'s apartment to say hello. When she came downstairs, she had a red leather jacket in her hand. She looked at me and said, 'Miles would have wanted you to have this'. I was stunned. I couldn't believe she was giving me this jacket. It was the fringed jacket that was in so many photographs and he wore it on his 1983 Grammy performance. It is one of my extremely treasured objects.

I read that you have a statue of Miles in your Paris home? What's it like and what made it right for your home?

Many years ago, when I was living in New Orleans, I bought a statue of Miles created by an African American sculptor named Ed Dwight. My parents had a piece of his when I was growing up, so I knew his work. When I later moved to Paris I had it shipped there and placed in the garden in the midst of beautiful greenery. So much of Miles' history is in Paris, so I love that his image is there with me watching over the house.

Do you have a favorite era of Miles' style that stood out for you or a favorite outfit that he wore that was memorable?

Miles had iconic looks in every era, but his look in the seventies really spoke to me. The leathers and suedes in rich earth tones.

What do you think his style said about him as an artist and as a man?

His style was an outer expression of his music and soul. It said this is me at this moment, but don't blink, 'cause it's gonna change in a minute.

What does your style say about you as an artist and as a man?

Exactly the same thing.

What is the most valuable thing you got from Miles, directly or inspirationally?

His music is the most valuable thing I got from him, but on a personal level, it was a compliment that I got from him about my first album, *Let Love Rule*. We happened to be on a flight together going from Los Angeles to New York and he saw me and came up to me. We hadn't seen each other in a minute, and he said that he was so proud of me and what I had done musically. That was a very deep moment for me because Miles did not bullshit. It was a gift of validation that brought everything back full circle to my childhood and my experience of witnessing him as this creative genius; And here he was digging my art.

If you had to describe him in a single word, what would it be?

'Mystical'.

Gersha Phillips is a costume designer for feature films and television. She has a long-standing work relationship with Don Cheadle, dating back to 1995 as a 'lowly wardrobe assistant' for 'Rebound: The Legend of Earl 'The Goat' Manigault', for HBO in 1996, up through and continuing on Cheadle's Showtime series, 'House of Lies'.

In this conversation, Gersha explains how she was brought on to one of her most challenging projects, 'Miles Ahead', working with Cheadle as not only the film's star but as a first time director and also the adventure of costuming an iconic, real-life character who during the period the movie was set had almost no real-life imagery available during the period the film was set in.

This is your fourth collaboration with Don Cheadle. How did you get onboard with 'Miles Ahead'?

When we worked together on 'Traitor', I had heard he was doing Miles Davis and told him I like him to consider me for costume designing the film. I had done 'Talk to Me' (also with Cheadle about a 70s era disc jockey) and I had some knowledge of the era. He told me then that I would be third in line behind Ruth Carter and Sharon Davis. Ruth was going to doing it, she was also in talks to do 'Selma', but she couldn't do them both, so she recommended me to Don, and he said he was already thinking of me, and that's how it happened. Ruth gave me the job! (laughs)

With Cheadle being not only the Star but also a first-time director, was your work process with him any different?

Very, very different. When I worked with him in the past, we would be talking about his character and what his character needed, etc. This was like talking about the whole film, and from a very different point of view, him as a director and what his vision was, based on the script, etc. and what had to happen. It was quite different, I must say. I think he enjoyed parts and didn't enjoy parts. (laughs)

What do you mean?

I just think he wasn't prepared totally for all of the questions that he would have to answer about everything. There's a lot of detail that goes into every department in film and those questions get answered by directors, depending on how involved they want to be. You have to navigate that relationship with them, so I'll have a better understanding of Don's process if we do it again.

What is your process when you start a new project?

I start with a lot of research. With Miles Davis, as you know the period, we were doing was very difficult. But we did a lot of flashbacks. So, we started somewhere in the mid to late fifties. We had flashbacks in the sixties, early seventies as well as seventy-nine, so there was quite a bit of research to do, based on Miles and the world around him. When I'm doing a period, I like to do a lot of research, collages on the wall, just as inspiration and also to get me thinking about what the silhouette should look like.

That's how I start, then I think about what I'm going to have to actually build and where I'm going to get my fabrics from. Fabrics are changing so much that it's harder and harder to reproduce fabrics accurately. Luckily, we were filming in Cincinnati and there was a guy who was a collector and had a massive amount of vintage clothes, especially in the late seventies and early eighties, which suited my period perfectly.

Don's things, we made a lot. We made all of his fifties things, even the things he wore in the seventies. Because of that era of Miles' life, there's not much imagery of it, we had to come up with ideas of what we thought it would be because he was always so fashion-forward, and so ahead of his time. He had a thing for Japanese designers, and I also looked at Italian designers, like Giorgio Armani. I also got some old (French male fashion magazine) l'Uomo Vogues and used those as prototypes for 1979. Even watching movies like *American Gigolo* and *Manhattan*, just to see what people were actually wearing. What you think of as the eighties is really late seventies. That was kind of a fun journey into the whole research process.

That's the research part. The next step is meetings with the director, finding out exactly what he wants. Then I draft a budget and see how much I can get away with building and how much I'll have to try to find somewhere. I think we built almost everything he (Don) wore, except for some shirts.

How involved did Don get with the wardrobe?

He was very involved. I showed him fabrics and colors because he was looking for a very specific, iconic Miles look. So, we went with a red silk shirt. In the main part of the movie in 1979, he wears two outfits, one is a robe thing that he has on when

Ewan McGregor's character comes to interview him. He wears that for a big part of it, so we found an Indian shawarma jacket from New York, so we remodeled and made it fit him. We couldn't afford to create what I wanted to build from scratch. He was very involved, even in what Ewan wore, because that was another outfit that had to last for a long period of time. They both wore two outfits for the whole movie.

How familiar were you with Miles prior to this project?

I knew about him from the fifties and sixties. There are some iconic images from those periods. And I knew about the eighties Miles, but I didn't know about the seventies. I was fascinated by that because there were so many amazing images and the way he dressed was pretty amazing, especially after he started dating Betty Davis. That relationship definitely had an impact on how he dressed. I just didn't know he was so funky! (laughs) I feel like from the late sixties until he dropped out in the mid-seventies, that was the best Miles to me. But the fifties and sixties, I quite loved the way he looked, but I didn't like his eighties style.

I tried to copy a suit of his, I think it was the late fifties, a gray suit, and I did it with a powder blue stripe through the gray. It's a high buttoned double-breasted but it's only got two buttons. It looked fabulous on him, and he looked so cool. He was doing some really interesting things, with fashion, with everything.

What were you going with regards to his look for this film?

Don Cheadle and Miles Davis are not the same physique, so that was something I had to come to terms with. Trying to replicate that look on Don's body and have it be as true to form as it needs to be. When you're paying homage to an icon, he's black, I'm black, I had a lot of different things going on, a lot of emotion, trying to do it and do it well, being trusted with such a great position. I was trying to achieve authenticity and serve Don's script. It's its own thing. It's not a biography, it's very different, so to find Miles in this world that we didn't know, we didn't see what he looked like, it's kind of like when he was a little down and out when the story starts. It's the sad part, but we wanted to do it in a way that's not offensive and also serve the story at the same time. We were trying to make it real, very honest.

Do you feel you like succeeded?

Y'know (laughs)…I think I succeeded for the time and budget I had to work with. You have to come to terms with the reality of what you're dealing with. If I had a larger budget with more time, in a city that had more to offer, it would have been a much different experience. But I was working on a low budget movie in Cincinnati with no time to work on it, with many different eras and these are the challenges we had to deal with.

I talked to Don about how he felt about it, and he expressed a similar thing. Money can really change the experience. But sometimes those limitations can result in amazing projects.

What was the outfit that stood out for you most from the film?

In 1960 something he (Don) got onstage in this really great blue suit and everything just sort of clicked. It was a little bit of a chill moment. It was really amazing. There was a particular outfit that I did, a turquoise color wool, with a shirt that was just off a shade of that and he wears it with chestnut shoes and a belt. It just looks amazing on him.

Was there anything in your experience on the film that surprised you about Miles?

The photo from the Gap ad, I always thought it was from the sixties and it was from the fifties? I thought it was much later than it was. He was innovative, a really, really, cool, cool guy. I don't know how he did that from where he came from. But he had some innate thing going on, where he was connecting on the next wave.

Percussionist, composer and producer **James Mtume** *played with Miles Davis from 1971 to 1975. Fiercely opinionated and hilarious, Mtume's time with Miles influenced his career when he segued into a successful career of writing and producing hits for artists like Stephanie Mills and Phyllis Hyman as well as a success career fronting his own funk-based band, Mtume, best known for their hit, 'Juicy Fruit'.*

Mtume discusses Miles' style, their relationship, his insomnia, his ability to translate abstract concepts into ideas that would open the minds of his players.

(MTUME) What a lot of people didn't understand, was every time he changed his music, he changed his look. You go back and look at those slick assed Italian suits from the sixties, the 'Milestones' cover and ultimate

go into 'Bitches Brew' and you will see an evolution of the look. He was beyond the music because he set trends, not just musically, but every time he changed the music, he changed the look, and everybody started dressing like him.

To be looking at a guy who spans the forties, all the way up to his death and you can see this amazing evolution. You can document each period of his music with a different look.

I think a great artist is always expressing himself, no matter what he does. For example, in addition to music, clothes and painting, I understand that Miles was also a great cook.

Brother was he ever! He and I would hang out and he would call me to come over for dinner and he would cook. He was a great cook. The guy that taught him was a jazz guy. He loved to cook; it was art to him. When I say he could cook, he could burn, baby!

What would you say was the best dish that he cooked for you?

Fish. Any kind of fish. The oils that he'd use...I'd watch him in the kitchen, and he'd treat that meal like he was creating a song. Checking his pots, very attentive. It was a gas to watch. First of all, he's got these slick assed clothes on and he's steady cookin'!

Anybody who thinks what you're doing is frivolous (writing this book) is missing the point. Here's a guy who set trends in fashion and achieved all of this while being a dark-skinned brother who was a sex symbol. Think about it, especially back then. Dark-skinned?! But he felt like he was a prince, and the whole world looked at him that way.

That's a very important element that we have to take into account. Miles was always aware (in the 1962 Playboy interview with Alex Haley) in most of the article, he's not talking about music, he's talking about white people and what it is to be black in America. No jazz artists talked about things like that, the way he did.

I saw it in many different circumstances. We played for ambassadors, kings, presidents and they all bowed, brother! He had an amazing presence; unlike anybody I'd ever been around. I mean, he's that, and then we'd turn around, get in his Ferrari and go uptown to a soul food restaurant.

How did you two meet?

I was playing with Freddie Hubbard down at the Vanguard, and Miles was in the audience checking it out. A couple of days later, I'm lying on the floor listening to music and the phone rings, and he said, 'hey, this is Miles'. I thought it was my friend N'dugu joking, so I said, 'quit bullshitin', and I hung up. A few seconds later, the phone rang again, 'MOTHERFUCKER, this is Miles! What are you doing for the next couple of months? I want you to join my band. We're going to Europe for four months'. That was it. His manager called and for the next five years, that's where I was at. I didn't see him again until it was time for rehearsal.

What was rehearsal like?

He wanted us to understand structure. I was a rehearsal freak. One day I said, 'Miles, we should rehearse more'. He told me, 'man, I pay you to rehearse on stage. 'I didn't quite understand it. He said, 'I want you to play what you don't know. If you over-rehearse, it's going to be familiar and the spontaneity won't be there'. It allowed you every night to explore something different. I remember one time he told me, 'what you don't play is more important than what you play'.

How long did it take for you to click with him musically?

Immediately. Immediately. The morning after the first concert in Germany, he called me and asked me to come to his suite. What he said brought tears to my eyes. He said, 'I ain't never felt nobody playing that under me, you're a thoroughbred'. That was the first gig and we were like that 'til the end.

What do you think made that musical relationship special?

I think because of our personal relationship. He said he saw a lot of himself in me as a young guy. I didn't take none of the bullshit and we would talk a lot late at night because I was an insomniac and so was he. So, he'd call me at four in the morning and we'd be talking about politics.

He called me, and I knew it was nobody but him. His first statement was, 'you ever see those samurai movies where they take an apple and lay it on somebody's neck and then take the sword and split the apple but not cut their throat? What if you could approach your instrument like that?' I said, 'what do you mean?' He said, 'the idea is that you're disciplined that you're barely touching it. I'm playing the trumpet, and I'm playing it so delicate, that the air is the sound.' I know it sounds crazy, but that's the stuff we would explore. My mind is opening up. Al those conversations and phrases, that gives you a whole new approach of how to approach music.

It seemed that he knew that even if he spoke abstractly, that you would get it, which gave room for a different kind of conversation.

It's incredible how much that excites your understanding, and how open everything can be. The intimacy that you learn to approach the music is on an existential level because you're approaching the music on levels that you would have never thought of. That's some other shit, man! When a band is clicking on that level, it's something that you can't explain.

I remember we were playing in Denver; we played for three hours. We got on the elevator, Miles laid down on the floor of the elevator and said, 'what the fuck was that?' We couldn't talk. Something had happened. Real talk and I'm not into spooking shit.

What it's like is this: you're exploring something, playing for two to three hours, there's a moment of ten or fifteen moments where there's this ecstasy and you're all on the same page. You become one mindset. It's just a special moment where you're not playing your instrument, your instrument is playing you. You're trying to figure out the best way you can contribute, which is to elevate.

There was a bass player, Miles tells him to come by and listen to the rehearsal outside. So, he does. We're inside playing, and Miles says, 'Mtume, he could never be in our band. 'I said, 'why'. He said 'any motherfucker that I tell to go sit outside and listen through the window (and he does it), he don't have the heart to be in this band. He should have told me, "fuck you". Playing music is eighty percent attitude, twenty percent technique. Most people think it's the other way around'.

Nobody else changed the complexion of music from the forties all the way through the seventies. That's just incomprehensible. Most great jazz musicians are remembered for a single composition. Monk: 'Round Midnight'. Dizzy: 'Night in Tunisia'. Duke Ellington: 'A-Train'. Look at all of the different compositions that we know Miles for. Different evolutions of the music. That's one thing I think about with these young jazz cats. You can't name me one standard song that any of them wrote, including Wynton Marsalis.

You mentioned Marsalis.

Fuck Wynton. But go ahead. (laughs)

I understand they had a pretty contentious relationship, how true is that?

No, THEY didn't, HE did. Miles never said nothing about him. He came under Stanley Crouch, that was his mentor. Crouch hates Miles. Wynton was so disrespectful, and the ultimate disrespect, he walked out onstage in New Orleans playing and never asked if he could sit in. Miles told me, 'I would never do that'. That was all part of that Stanley Crouch extension and Wynton buying into that shit, thinking he was the baddest motherfucker because he was playing European jazz, never knowing that Clifford Brown was doing that shit thirty years before he was born.

How did you apply lessons learned when you started your own solo career?

I always had a good sense of melody. When I started my own band, I was experimenting with how to reduce everything to its highest common denominator. 'Simplexicity'. That's what I call it. An outgrowth of knowing how he would abbreviate. Learn how to make the statement. Fuck the paragraph. Get to the essence. I could take the notes I don't need out.

When you think about Miles and his style, what comes to mind?

He dressed like he played. Whatever it was, it was always the slickest shit for that time. He had no corners in his house. They were all smooth because he didn't like corners. Every slick dude saw a part of himself in Miles. And how to be proud and black. His grandfather was a Garveyite, so that's where that came from.

What about Miles do you think people would find surprising if they knew?

The thing that was most special to me, was Miles was the best friend you could have because 'yes' was 'yes' and 'no' was 'no'. But brother, if he didn't dig you, you didn't worry about where he was at. Vibes. He told me, 'I can tell if a motherfucker can play by the way he takes his horn out'.

When was the last time you saw him?

For years, he would invite to me his birthday parties at Tavern on the Green in New York, but I was always out of town. Cicely Tyson called me and said he's having a party and that I needed to come, so I did, and it was great. Then he was dead a few months later.

If you could describe Miles in one word, what would it be?

'Future'. He was always looking to the future.

Plucked from Stevie Wonder's touring band at the age of 19 by Miles Davis himself,
Michael Henderson *carved out a successful career as a premier bassist. He made it a huge career backing a variety of stars during the Motown glory days, as a sideman for Miles Davis form 1970 -77 and a featured vocalist for Norman Connors on several classic R&B tunes: 'You are My Starship' and the self-penned 'Valentine Love', before embarking on a memorable career as a solo artist, striking gold with 'In the Night Time' and 'Wide Receiver'. Henderson recently toured with a Miles Davis tribute shows entitled 'Electric Miles'. As a young DJ in the '80s, Michael was kind enough to give me my first radio interview, so it was a special treat to talk with him again. By the way, he does an eerily perfect impersonation of Miles.*

What were you doing when you met Miles?

I was recording with Stevie Wonder in the UK. We had just finished 'Top of the Town' and was heading to New York to do the Apollo and a club date. Miles came down to the club and he was dressed! He was with Betty Davis.

Do you remember what outfit he had on?

I think it was suede pants, the boots were sort of patchwork, green, red, silver, a suede jacket, silk shirt and sunglasses. Betty Davis was dressed pretty much like Miles was. Betty knew Jimi (Hendrix) and during that time we were all into leather, suede and snakeskin. We had people that were making the clothes for us. I even had a kangaroo maxi coat. That was the fashion at that time.

When Miles came to the show, was he coming to see you?

Betty Davis brought him to see me, because he was looking to change his music and he wanted a new style for his band, so she brought him to see me.

So, you knew Betty?

No, I didn't know Betty. She knew of me because of Stevie Wonder, Aretha and all of the people I'd worked with. Mick Jagger, Stokely Carmichael and Angela Davis were all there that night. It was something!

How long was it before he approached you about joining the band?

He came right up to the dressing room. He walked up to Stevie and said in his raspy voice, 'nice to meet you, I'm taking your fuckin' bass player'. I don't think Steve really heard him, but he was serious. Sometime later at the Apollo Theater, I was at a rehearsal in the basement with the Rueben Phillips Band, Miles comes in, dressed again. Maxi coat, he wore those dashiki beads, that kind of stuff, silk shirt and leather pants. When he walked in, the whole band froze.

I was back in the corner. He walked all the back there and gave me his phone number and told me to call him.

What happened right after that?

He flew me (from Detroit) into New York, to his house, we had a rehearsal and he showed me his closet. His bedroom was like the Starship Enterprise! The closet was full of suede and leather. All kinds of belts made out of various materials, sunglasses, all kinds of stuff. Just really unbelievable. Nobody dressed like that back then.

Was there a particular outfit worn by Miles that has been etched in your mind?

No, because he always had something new made. He always was coming with something new. Do you hear me? (laughs) I don't think I ever saw him wear the same thing twice. He had a tailor; he had a guy who made his hats and bags for him. He had a hairdresser, James Finney. James Finney did Jimi Hendrix's hair, Jimi's hair didn't just look like that on its own. He did Ashford & Simpson's hair; on occasion he'd do my hair. He was the fashion guy who kept Miles' hair together.

How did working with Miles affect your personal style?

I was wearing suits and some kangaroo coats before I got with Miles. I had some suedes and some leathers, but I had to up my status with Miles. I had to do the upgrade because he was so sharp. You'd have to step your game up.

Did he give you any tips, or he let you pick whatever suits your personality?

Well, when you saw Miles, you got a lot of ideas! All you had to do was open your eyes and see.

We were in Italy walking around, up in the hills at a ski resort. There were some glasses in a window. We went up to get the glasses, I put the glasses on, and Miles said, 'they'd be a motherfucker if you take the rubber off the rim'. So, we bought the glasses and took the rubber off and those are some of the glasses you'd see him wearing. I started wear them too, then they started manufacturing the glasses like that without the rubber on them. (*Michael is wearing a pair of the glasses in question on the cover of his debut solo album, 'Solid'.*)

All the women were incredible. They wore see-through tops with leather pants, 'big afros, beautiful and fresh and sexy. A clean look. Betty Davis, I'd never seen anybody like her. When she showed up, Oh My God! Everything was beautiful. Those leather pants...that's how beautiful she was. I mean even Stevie Wonder could see her!

How tall was Miles?

He was 5 something. I'm 6'6" and he came up to my shoulders, so 5'7, 5'8.

How would you describe your relationship with him?

We hit it off and it was almost like a father and son, and a friend too. He was just the best. Everything he did, he took care of business. He always took care of me. Some people I worked with, weren't so cool, but he was one of the best. Gladys Knight, Aretha Franklin, they always took care of business, and Miles Davis is right up there with them.

What do you think his clothes say about him as a person and as an

artist?

It shows confidence and power. That he's a serious, confident man, and a spiritual person. The colors he wore, when he put these certain clothes on, he had a different swagger going on. He held his head high. You could see the confidence in him. He looked good, so he played good. Everything was good. He could cook good. I remember the white fish gumbo he used to make. He could always surprise you with the new clothes that he had made. Every time the band saw him, we'd say 'wooo!' He always liked that. He would go out of his way to make you say 'wooo!' He was always sharp, even going through the airport.

Did he ever compliment you on your personal style?

If he saw me with some nice shit on, he'd say 'Hey Michael, aw shit! You lookin' kinda fly and shit. Go 'head, Michael, go 'head!' He inspired me to free my style up from suits and ties, to just get loose.

In the 70s, he started wearing those big glasses I was talking about. Nobody was wearing those. When I started wearing them, people would ask me 'are you the Green Hornet' or something?

What particular era of his clothes did you like the best?

I like the time that I was with him. The music had changed, the war was going on, music was fresh. At the same time, I was working with Miles, I was working with Marvin Gaye, and I had just left Stevie Wonder. In 1971-1972, Marvin Gaye was changing, his clothes were evolving, and I was working with both of them! This was a helluva time. It seemed like everything changed in the world and he was ahead of all of it.

How would you describe Miles Davis in a single word?

Miles Davis in one word? A male 'Oracle'. You know like in 'The Matrix', the woman who knew everything. That's Miles Davis.

MILESSTYLE

6. WE WANT MILES: 1981-1991

'You can't always believe what Miles says, but you can always believe what he plays'.

-Marcus Miller

In an interview with Leonard Feather, Miles Davis infamously derided the value of family: "I don't believe in families. Like, if I die, my money ain't goin' to people just because they're close relatives". Like many other uncensored statements made over the years, the idea was a big contradiction to the reality of the man. In fact, it was his connection to his family that helped him through his toughest times, brought him back into the light, helped reclaim his passion for music and also led him to finally let his guard down (as much as someone like Miles Davis ever could).

Miles was still in seclusion when the eighties arrived, bringing with it an upheaval of cultural change. Disco was winding down, while hip-hop was heating up. Fusion was still banging around, with stalwarts like Lenny White, Stanley Clarke and Weather Report was still driving the music, but moving towards a more melodic, rhythm-based, accessible sound.

Rock music's identity continued to fray, as established acts like The Rolling Stones, David Bowie and Rod Stewart were segueing out of the short-lived dance craze, back to more traditional pop-rock confections, while the British based new wave trend wound up short lived, but influential.

In America, R&B was still a powerful force that hadn't yet consistently topped the pop charts, but artists like Michael Jackson, Prince, Lionel Richie and Whitney Houston were making it difficult to keep pop 'pure'. Bruce Springsteen was leading the charge of US-based rock, while artists like Madonna, Eurythmics and Hall & Oates were perfecting the art of the pop hit single, with million-seller after million-seller.

Along with music, fashion found a new foothold by marrying the latest styles with the hottest music, via the explosive new communication breakthrough, the music video. MTV's arrival quickly connected fans to their favorite artists in ways they had never experienced before. The 24 hour a day music channel crossed the Atlantic and brought the excitement of Britain's New Wave of aggressive, sometimes violent, always rebellious music to American living rooms, while simultaneously introducing US music lovers to the smoother, subtle sounds of the New Romantics trend, typified by groups like Spandau Ballet, Japan, The Thompson Twins, Adam and the Ants and hundreds more.

In the midst of all of this activity, Miles Davis was tentatively taking his first real steps out of the Brownstone on West 77th St.

After a couple of unsuccessful attempts at getting his creative juices flowing, Miles' sister Dorothy who was alerted concerning his horrific physical deterioration by composer/arranger Paul Buckmaster, reached out to his former intimate, actress Cicely Tyson, for help. Tyson quickly made dramatic moves that might have actually saved the life of the embattled legend.

Tyson got rid of all of the coping mechanisms and negative influences surrounding Davis. She was able to get him to cut back on his alcohol consumption and got him off drugs. According to Miles, from his autobiography, "She kind of protected me and started seeing that I ate the right things. She turned me on to acupuncture to help get my hip back in shape. All of a sudden I started thinking clearer, and that's when I really started thinking about music again" (*autobiography, pg. 340*).

In 1980, Dorothy's son, drummer Vincent Wilburn Jr., started playing him tunes over the phone that his band had created in Chicago, which rekindled his interest in his one true love; music. Shortly thereafter, Miles began playing with Vincent and his young band, but it was a slow return to form. In poor health and with an out of shape embouchure (the facial muscles and shape of the lips used on the mouthpiece of the trumpet); the legend struggled to find his footing. However, he forged on, and his comeback album, *The Man with the Horn*, released in 1981, was ultimately as indistinct as the record's title. But the important thing was that he was back to music, and on a healthier path than he had been on in years.

Following the release of *The Man with the Horn*, Miles went through several iterations of band members until he assembled what he felt was the perfect group that he wanted in order to test his comeback on the road. Key among all members was bassist Marcus Miller, who would end up composing and producing several of his final albums.

As the eighties wore on, Miles began to find his footing both creatively and personally. While *The Man with the Horn* was universally pronounced a major disappointment by most critics, the resulting tour sold well and yielded a commercially and critically successful live album, *We Want Miles*.

During this rebirth, Miles' health continued to be deteriorate. In 1982, he had a stroke, which left him weak, and in his words "I looked like death waiting to eat a soda cracker" (*autobiography, pg. 350*). He slowly regained his strength and stamina but lost the bulk of his hair and began wearing a weave, which eventually gave way to a curly flowing wig that looked like an arrangement that wouldn't have been out of place during the time of Henry VIII.

As ever, Miles' interest in clothes continued to evolve and move into what would become his most flamboyant period, and that too was saying something.

When Miles initially came back to performing live, it wasn't uncommon to see him in a loose-fitting one-piece jumpsuit, with a pair of clogs and a knit skull cap. Given that his health was still unstable, and his physical state was fragile, this type of dressing was more comfortable, and beyond that, it was loose and easy to slip in and out of, which was equally was low maintenance.

However, when his health improved and his strength returned, along with his curiosity and love of the spotlight, he embraced the style of the eighties wholeheartedly. Linebacker shoulder pads, genie pants, leather, silk, metal fabrics, nothing was too outrageous. To describe his look as an intergalactic, rock star pimp would be putting it too lightly and watering down the impact. Japanese designers like Issey Misyake, Koshin Satoh and Eiko Ishioka, who designed the artwork for the 'Tutu' album, captured his imagination. Miles was being feted around the world as both a legend and rock star. He dressed the part.

Miles kept his eyes open for new trends in clothing, the same way he chased fresh approaches in music. When his assistant Mikel Elam kept showing up to work in unique trendy attire, Miles would ask him where he got his clothes. When Mikel would repeatedly reply "Patrick Bushnell", Miles made a mental note to go and check him out, and eventually at some point he had Patrick start creating outfits for him too.

Mikel said that as picky as Miles was about his outfits, he didn't take very good care of them. "He was like a little kid with his clothes. They were incredible on Monday, forgotten on Friday. 'What's next?' He would paint in his clothes, eat in them, and get 'em messed up. He had so many, that would give him an excuse to wear something different."

This outer space persona was an interesting contrast in Miles' personal evolution. It seemed as he began opening up more in interviews, engaging with the public and sharing more of himself, he began to almost bury himself under layers and layers of oversized exotic outfits, from the thick curly helmet on his head, to the pitch-black shades that nearly covered his face, to the outfits that were draped so large and dramatically, one could barely see the artist inside. Perhaps he felt it necessary to build a sort of protective armor because of his inconsistent health. Maybe because he was beginning to show so much of his heart that this last stylistic turn was his way of keeping something for himself. Or perhaps, he just liked looking like no one else on Earth.

In 1985, Miles released his final album for Columbia, *You're Under Arrest*. It featured a striking album cover photo by Anthony Barboza, featuring Miles in all black, looking like either Zorro or a new wave gangster, a stern look on his face, and cradling a toy machine gun. Notable for ending a professional association that spanned nearly forty years, *You're Under Arrest* also yielded two of the most popular songs of his career while raining down hellfire from jazz purists.

Cyndi Lauper's pop ballad *Time After Time* and Michael Jackson's *Human Nature* both showcased Miles' facility of marrying simple melodies that resonate with emotional power. His deep sensitivity could be felt in every note hit in *Time After Time*: soft, steady playing that conveyed understanding and compassion. *Human Nature* showed a more playful, yet sympathetic approach that conveyed the light airiness of Davis' approach, one that urged the listener to embrace the warmth and ambiance of this contemporary classic pop song.

Critics hated the two songs, arguing that they were both beneath him, while young up and coming trumpeter Wynton Marsalis repeatedly dismissed Miles' comeback as uninspired and continued to berate him in public. Miles was initially disappointed, but then that spanned into anger as he expressed his displeasure that the young man whose talent he respected refused to return the same regard to his much more established elder, but as always, Miles refused to let the criticism veer him from his singular path, regardless of where the critiques came from.

Davis found a welcome new home at Warner Bros. Records, where they supported his forays into more contemporary sounds, encouraging collaborations with pop stylists Chaka Khan, Prince, Scritti Politti and Cameo, adventurous technical ventures via programmed synthesizers, drum loops and sampling, with Marcus Miller manning the ship. The initial result, *Tutu*, didn't endear him to traditional jazz critics, but opened his music up to a wider audience and also yielded him a Grammy Award for Best Jazz Instrumental Performance. He also lent his musical voice to the protest album, *Artists Against Apartheid*, featuring U2, George Clinton, Afrika Bambatta and a host of other popular musicians from around the world.

His commercial success and iconic status did not only improve him as an artist, but Miles was more in demand than ever before. He was selling out concert tickets around the world. His tours paid him like a rock star, and in that time, he decided to scratch an acting itch, appearing in cutting edge television shows like *Miami Vice* and *Saturday Night Live*, while also appearing on the big screen in *Dingo*, an Australian film about a young jazz aficionado who travels to Europe to meet his idol, legendary trumpet player, Billy Cross (Davis). While he was far from memorable with regards to acting, Miles turned out to be very comfortable on camera and he often shows a softer and more vulnerable side in his dealings with his loyal supporter. Unfortunately, Miles died before it was released.

He did more soundtrack work, *Street Smart* (starring Christopher Reeve and featuring the career breakthrough performance of Morgan Freeman), *The Hot Spot*, directed by Dennis Hopper, starring Don Johnson, Jennifer Connelly and Virginia Madsen. He also did the soundtrack for *Siesta*, starring Ellen Barkin, produced by Marcus Miller. Miles dedicated the album to his great friend Gil Evans, who died in 1988 following a long illness.

Personally, Davis continued to stretch out, marrying Cicely Tyson at Bill Cosby's home in 1981, moving to Malibu, eating healthy foods, using swimming as a replacement for boxing and embracing a new creative outlet, painting. He also found the time to complete his hotly contested autobiography, *Miles: The Autobiography*, co-authored with Quincy Trope.

Miles: The Autobiography was an immediate bestseller and like most things related to Miles Davis, highly controversial. While Miles was forthcoming about his drug use and abuse towards women, many believed and rumored that he 'borrowed' liberally from other pre-existing biographies about him, twisted the truth on some events and straight-up lied about others. The item that has haunted his legacy more than anything else in the book and continues to cast a dark cloud over him in some corners is his admittedly shameful violence against women. In the book he acknowledges that his past behavior was inexcusable, and voices regret for his actions, but regardless of his contriteness, this unfortunate behavior has already become a permanent part of his legacy.

Miles continued spending more time talking and engaging in a way he'd never done before. He did more interviews and appeared more on television, being profiled on *60 Minutes*, doing eccentric interviews on the *Today Show* and *Arsenio Hall* among others. Japanese television commercials was another part of his portfolio, at some point, as was appearing on fashion show runways, once with Andy Warhol obediently following him, keeping Miles' flowing cape from dragging on the runway floor.

Miles continued touring and recording until nearly the end of his life. Alternately enrapturing fans and infuriating critics, Davis capped his recording career with a pioneering effort of fusing hip hop with jazz on the well-intentioned but ultimately inadequate *Doo-Bop*, and a return to the days of his partnership with Bill Evans on the Quincy Jones helmed *Miles & Quincy: Live at Montreux*, recorded at the legendary jazz festival in Switzerland.

Although the final decade was among the most productive and healthiest of his adult life, Miles continually struggled with a variety of maladies and ailments that never totally abated. Compounded by his constant touring and various activities, his system ran down and finally wore out.

Miles played the Montreux concert in July; his final concert was at the Hollywood Bowl in August and he had taken ill shortly thereafter. He got worse and never recovered from that illness. Miles Davis died on September 29, 1991. A store was reported as the official cause of death, along with pneumonia and respiratory failure. His companion at the time, Jo Gelbard said in an interview with George Cole, "he was dying - he knew it and I knew it. His choice in the last year of his life was to almost accelerate the process because he worked tremendously. He was painting a lot, he did this whole tour, he was recording, so he made almost a conscious choice to live his life full pressure until it was no longer possible."

After changing the face of music more than once, reinventing himself personally and professionally countless times, burning with an endless curiosity that led him down and through many a bumpy road, Miles Davis earned his final rest and leaves a complicated legacy. A legacy that continues to grow and reach new fans around the world, whether it be for his music, his paintings, his personal style or his commitment to self, while also being challenged for his personal failings, his sometime questionable creative endeavors and his "I do what I want" attitude.

A true artist's story rarely comes in simple black and white, and whatever one is left with when considering the complexity of Miles Davis, his huge impact on fashion as it concerns musicians and the fashion industry in general, cannot be downplayed or overemphasized. Also, Miles' legitimacy as one of the most important artists of the last hundred years is without question.

'Anybody can play. The note is only 20 percent. The attitude of the motherfucker who plays it is 80 percent'. – Miles Davis

We Want Miles
CONVOS

MILESSTYLE

Issey Miyake is a renowned fashion designer from Hiroshima, Japan. In addition to his avant-garde, cutting edge sense of design, Miyake-san also created the late Steve Jobs' iconic black turtleneck sweater, providing him with over 100 for his personal use.

It's not surprising that during the last decade of his life, that Miles Davis became enamored with clothes made by Issey Miyake. The designer, like Miles, is known for pushing the boundaries of his profession, experimenting with unlikely textiles, shapes and fabric technology to create garments that would make a statement. He is clearly a leader and not a follower, not unlike Miles. If you replace 'clothing' with 'music' in the following quote from Miyake-san, it reads like a description of Miles Davis: 'Function alone does not make clothing appealing. We yearn for the beautiful, the unknown and the mysterious'.

Miyake-san's empire continues to do brisk business while he enjoys semi-retirement in Japan. He was kind enough to provide the author with an exclusive statement on his regard and appreciation for Miles Davis.

'Like all fans of Miles Davis, I followed his music from the time I was a student. As a result, it was a special thrill when I heard that he was wearing clothing he'd purchased from my stores in Paris, London or NY. I never made anything special for him. However, I do know that he really loved one leather jacket, which I saw him wearing often in photos. Eventually, I was introduced to him in NY and it was thrilling to connect this cool man to his music, especially that amazing album *Birth of the Cool*. I have a photo of him that I cherish, taken by William Coupon for the Japanese magazine DANSEN.

If I were to describe Miles in a single word, it would be 'Fierce'.'

Groove and rhythm were critical components of Miles Davis' music, especially in the later years of his career. One of the anchors of one of his latter-day bands was **Darryl Jones**, *an incredible bassist who also did tours of duty with Sting, Herbie Hancock, Madonna and Eric Clapton among others, and has been holding it down with the Rolling Stones in the studio and on the road since 1993. At 21, with the help of childhood friend (and nephew of Miles Davis) Vincent Wilburn, Jr., Darryl joined Miles band for five years and never looked back.*

What was your first impression when you met Miles face to face?

Honestly man, he was really funny! He immediately set about kind of trying to relax the situation. On my way up in the elevator I was chewing gum and he asked me for a stick. I said, 'actually man this is my last piece.'

And he goes, 'you mean you came all the way to New York and you only bought one piece of  gum?' I don't know, for some reason I wasn't really nervous. But the thing that was really kind that he said to me before I even pulled my bass out was, 'listen, if this doesn't work out it doesn't mean that you can't play, it just means that I'm looking for something else.' For a guy who realized the magnitude of his decision, I thought it was incredibly kind of him to take that kind of care of me before I even played.

What do you think made you a good fit for what he was going after musically at that time?

I grew up in a family where my dad was listening to early Miles and Oscar Peterson and Count Basie, but my mom was listening to Sly Stone and James Brown and Curtis Mayfield, so I kind of grew up realizing the importance of learning how to play jazz but also being exposed to the music of my time, which was like Sly and Jimi Hendrix. I think that the mixture of those two, having at least a basic understanding of jazz and growing up at the time that I did was helpful. There was kind of a bass revolution going on with Stanley Clarke and Larry Graham I think that that that prepared me for this situation.

Did it take very long for you to gel with what he was doing, or did you guys fall into a groove pretty quickly?

He told me that he was going to try me out at one price, and he said, 'we'll see how that works for a few weeks and if I feel like everything's working out, then you'll know in a few weeks or a month'. He said at some point in the future 'I'll take you up to the to the price the rest of the band is making'. I think we did two or three gigs and he pulls me into his dressing room after the gig and says, 'so I'm taking you to full pay'.

What about Miles that surprised you?

One of the things that comes to mind was that he was he was funny. He had a really great sense of humor. I didn't expect that. I expected a real, real serious person and he was, when it came to the music. But in a social kind of way, he was just funny with his observations of things.

You were playing with him when he was into his most flamboyant phase of dressing well. What do you remember about that?

I thought it was as exciting if not more than the stuff he had been wearing before. I guess it started really in the seventies, when he stopped wearing suits. It was pretty far out, going to snakeskin pants and boots and the glasses were always real cutting edge. I even heard once that him and Sly Stone were in a contest to see who could wear the hippest stuff. If you look at them, they're both really cutting edge, late sixties, early seventies. Then in the mid-eighties, he was making some pretty bold statements and I thought it was great.

I always thought it was it was an interesting contrast because if you look back to the fifties and sixties when he was wearing the Ivy League look and then the segue into the Italian style, the music was really more cutting edge and aggressive, kind of pioneering and then in the last ten years while he was still pioneering, it was arguably a lot more accessible to general consumers while his visual style was a lot more aggressive and unique.

That's interesting. I hadn't really thought about that, but you are right in that respect. Although at the point that he was wearing the Ivy League stuff that was a pretty new statement for a black man. I think that was in its way, cutting edge. I don't think blacks were really exposed very much to the Ivy League look at that time, so for him to have chosen that was again a bit of a statement as well as the Italian thing, was before everybody got into Italian clothes. As always, he was a little bit ahead of the pack.

One of the things that inspired me to write the book is that it just seemed like he was such a complete artist in everything did, whether it was music or painting or clothes and I understand he was also a spectacular cook. His whole essence seemed to be an expression as an artist.

I asked him about cooking, and he said, 'Darryl, one art helps the other.' He was also drawing a lot at that time, even a little bit before he started painting, he'd use a lot of color pencils and color pens right before he started using canvas and paint. He just felt like it was all the same thing. When I speak about his sense of humor, it wasn't like he would just tell you a joke, it's like you would see something and he would comment on it and it had that same kind of high level creative outlook and that was what was so funny about him.

In all areas of his life there was always a creative flair to it. When you talk about Miles, it's really much more style than it is something like fashion. It is a kind of way of life for him. He would he would slide the saltshaker over to you on the table, but then he would find a different way to pass you the pepper. There was always something creative about the way that he was doing anything. I remember telling him once that when I walked out on stage and my pants were too short or too long that I couldn't really play. It made me self-conscious about the way I'm playing because I would look down and something wasn't right. He just immediately said 'exactly!' It's one of those things where you're trying to do this creative thing that requires you to be conscious of the musicians around you, so the moment that something takes away from that you've got to fix that before you get on stage. It was one of those things that we really shared. He said, 'man, if I look down and everything doesn't look just a certain way, I can't play right.'

Did Miles ever give you any fashion advice?

I bought this Francois Girbaud outfit, who was huge at the time. Everybody was getting into the Girbaud pants. It was a jumpsuit by Girbaud, a nice outfit, kind of pleated pants and a safari kind of top, it was all one piece. I was wearing oxblood colored shoes with it and Miles said, 'you could actually wear black shoes with that' and I said 'blue and black shoes, that doesn't work for me. I don't really like that. Whenever I wear blue, I tend to wear brown shoes or shoes that are not black.' He immediately backed up and said, 'Oh, ok! I don't mean to step on your sensibility!' It was one of those things where whenever I wear a blue color, if I'm wearing gray or from black then I wear a black shoe. But black shoes to me, they really stop something when you wear and with other color clothes. And he just looked at me like 'damn, you got it as bad as I do!'

Is there any particular era of his music that resonates with you the most?

I'd have to say all of it. I was in the car the other day and I made a playlist right quick and 'Old Devil Moon' came up. That is one of the quintessential Miles songs. The solo I can sing in my sleep, everything that he plays on that. I know it by heart, and I know it by heart because my father was playing that music when I was a two-year old. That's like bread and butter for me. 'Round Midnight' is another record that I just I know in a way that that surpasses my musical history. So, there's all of that stuff but when we started doing *Decoy*, I thought that that was an incredible direction and I thought that he would go kind of in that direction for a while, but he didn't.

I remember him asking me 'you know that Cyndi Lauper tune *Time After Time*? Learn that. We're gonna play that.' I remember thinking now he wants to play pop tunes now that I'm in the band, without realizing he's been doing that his whole career. So, to say that I have one period that's my favorite, I can't say. I'm thinking about the *Bitches Brew* period, I love the stuff that he did with Marcus, I think it's really amazing. I don't have a favorite really. I was just listening to some of that *Birth of the Cool* stuff. it's just everything.

The music is where it starts but so many years after his death why do you think there continues to be so much fascination about Miles Davis?

I just think he was an incredibly independent thinker and there was a lot of media access and I think that with the world having changed in the way that it has become more media centric he's a natural candidate for people to want to know more about him. He's just one of those guys, they don't make a lot of them. They don't make a lot of guys who are really independent thinkers, who are going to go their own way, regardless of the consequences.

When was the last time you saw him?

The last time I saw Miles he played in Chicago I think about 4 or 5 days before the Hollywood Bowl concert, which was the last concert that he played. I saw him at that concert and then I went up to his hotel room and spoke with him. He asked why he hadn't heard anything from me, why I hadn't done a record on my own. Before I could answer, he said, 'oh yeah. You're one of them'. I said, 'one of what?' He said 'perfectionist'. He said, 'Darryl, you play the bass perfect. The only thing you need to do is take other musicians who you admire, put what they do with what you do, and it will be perfect'.

He had told me he was having some health issues, but right as I got to the door he said, 'you be safe on your way home, 'cause you know you're still my bass player.' I looked at him and said, 'of course I am and of course I'll always be'. That was actually the last thing he said to me.

If you could describe him in one word what would it be?

To actually to reduce Miles to one word is not possible really. Everybody talks about him being a genius and I totally agree, but he worked hard at it because he loved it and getting it right was of such importance to him. But I have to say that I've never met anybody who love music more than Miles.

Dr. Todd Boyd- aka 'The Notorious Ph.D.', is the Katherine and Frank Price Endowed Chair for the Study of Race and Popular Culture and Professor of Cinema and Media Studies in the USC School of Cinematic Arts. Dr. Boyd offered expert commentary in a documentary about the classic blaxploitation film 'Super Fly'. He graciously did the same in a recent documentary about the original 'Shaft' trilogy, 'A Complicated Man', which is where I met him. During a break in the interview, I discovered that he has a deep love and appreciation for Miles Davis, and he agreed to share a few thoughts about Miles' cultural impact through his music and image.

When did Miles Davis first come onto your radar?

I would say with my father. It started with my dad talking about Miles with his friends. Whenever his name would come up on television or in the newspaper or something like that, my father had a reaction to it, so that's where it started.

Can you remember any particular song, album or image where Miles really made a serious impression on you?

When I was a kid back in the seventies, we'd be in the car and my father was always upset that the local radio station (jazz formatted WJZZ, Detroit) was not playing what he considered 'real' jazz anymore and he would often blame Miles. He's like, 'Miles started playing that bullshit and now everybody's playing bullshit'. It would be a response like that which was kind of funny to me. But as I got older, I understood it. He was really animated about this. And then he and his friends would talk about Miles. I remember this one conversation he had with a really close friend of his, and they were both saying 'fuck Miles' and I'm like 'whoa! What is that about?' They were really critical. I didn't get it because this guy Miles Davis is supposed to be the real deal and my father and his friend talked about him like he ain't shit.

That criticism of Miles made me curious that there was this guy who generated this kind of response from my father, who was indifferent about a lot of things. So, I started investigating on my own. This is in the eighties and Miles is playing 'Time After Time' and 'Human Nature'. He's playing pop songs and I'm kind of confused further. And my father's like 'you didn't hear Miles when he was really blowing', like he stopped blowing and started to play bullshit. It was around this time that (Wynton) Marsalis started to become really visible and he's a guy from my generation who was saying the same kind of things my father was saying. I made it an effort to study Miles to find out for myself why he generated all this conversation.

But where do you start? 'Round Midnight' (the film) had come out a couple years earlier with Dexter Gordon and is one of my favorite films. I'm going through albums (at the record store) I see Miles and this album called '*Round about Midnight* so that that's where it started. I liked what I heard, so I went back and bought *Someday My Prince Will Come*. Not too long after this Miles' autobiography came out and I started reading it. As I'm reading it, I thought 'this is what I need, because I'm going to get a list of these albums so that I can go deal with him accordingly. That's what got me started.

What do you think that Miles met to black people during his time and since his passing?

He was a new type of celebrity for black culture. When he blew up in the late fifties, things were changing rapidly, and Miles was very vocal about not wanting to be seen as an entertainer. He wanted to be seen as an artist. There was this need to break away from a cat like 'Pops' Louis Armstrong, who came from a different generation and had a very different way of doing it.

So, here's Miles and he's many things. He's a great artist, he's putting out these hot albums. And even though a lot of people really aren't listening to jazz they know who he is. He has a glamorous marriage to this dancer in Frances, he's known for how well dressed he is, his lifestyle, where he lives, who he hangs out with. And then with his whole persona, he was the embodiment of 'cool' as a style at a time when this became an aesthetic unto itself.

Here's this dark-skinned black man at this particular moment in time who makes it clear he's not gonna take any shit off anybody. He's even kind of confrontational in that way. And this is the era when the Nation of Islam emerges. This is the era when eventually Muhammed Ali emerged and it's the era of a new style of black masculinity. Eventually Miles would be married to Cicely Tyson. He pissed white people off because he wasn't going to play the role that society had assigned him to.

So, I think for a lot of black people, even if they didn't know much about his music, they knew the name, they recognized his stardom and there was an appreciation for what he represented.

I think you can draw a straight line from what Miles is doing then to what the Black Panthers would be doing ten years or so later in the late sixties. His whole persona certainly resonates in hip hop culture so many years later. He had the image of the strong black man who was not afraid to speak truth to power, who was not afraid to talk about racism, but who also lived this really glamorous life.

I always say to people Miles was driving a Ferrari when there really weren't that many foreign cars in the country and a lot of black people couldn't even get a drink of water. So, when you think about the emphasis the culture has put on success, Miles was a shining example of success before there were a lot of other (black) people who could claim the same thing.

You said in a in a great article on theroof.com that 'cool detached from its history is style without substance in the worst way'. You mentioned cool pioneers like Duke Ellington, Billy Eckstine and Lester Young, but Miles seems to be the ongoing embodiment of cool more than the other folks that you mention. Why do you think that is?

To me it's generational. Duke, Prez, Mr. B, those guys were from a different generation. Miles is younger than they were, and they did what they did based on what was available to them at that time. Miles learned from them. He appropriated a lot from Billy Eckstine. He talks about that openly. Miles comes along at a time when things were changing, and he was able to absorb what those guys were doing and then direct it in a different way. He's got a major record label behind him once he goes to Columbia and this is the heyday of magazines in a way, certainly magazine photography. So, when you start to think about album covers and photos in magazines, it just wasn't happening in the culture. The very first Playboy interview is Alex Haley interviewing Miles and Playboy was a relatively new magazine at the time.

I would say late fifties to the late sixties, early seventies 'cool' became something that was visible in society and it was controversial. People now use that word 'cool' to mean anything. It almost doesn't have a meaning. But back then to be 'cool' relative to the mainstream society was considered negative; emotionally detached, people associated with anger, a lot of people associated with heroin usage, etc. Black jazz musicians were not universally embraced or accepted. There was a segment of people who listen to the music, but those people were hip. The masses didn't know anything about it and a lot of information was really misinformation.

Miles represents all of that. *Birth of the Cool* is an album that he lived in the way he carried himself. It was more than just style. It wasn't just some stylist taking him shopping and buying him some nice clothes. When he put those clothes on, he really wore them. They didn't just hang off his body. The way he carried himself, some of it is conscious. It's just the way he is. He embodies this ethos. He wears it, he defines it. He is it.

He was strongly influenced by Sugar Ray Robinson, one of the coolest cultural figures ever. There are so many people that he absorbed; he talks about how Fred Astaire influenced the way he wanted to dress. Most people wouldn't make that association, but that's what you do as a jazz musician, you take all this information and flip it through your instrument. Miles was doing that with his instrument, but he was also doing that with his life.

Is there an era of his fashion that particularly resonates with you?

When he's wearing suits, certainly. For me it starts with those Prestige albums: *Workin'*, *Cookin' Steamin'* and *Relaxin'*. If you look at what he's wearing on those album covers and then he goes over to Columbia, the green shirt on the album (*Milestones*) cover is famous, but then you start to see suede jackets and suit and tie combos. Then you get to this period (which is my favorite) mid to late sixties, when he gets his younger band with Herbie Hancock, Ron Carter, Tony Williams, Wayne Shorter and those guys. They're playing a lot and in Europe. If you ever see footage of some of those concerts, Miles is so clean and it's so minimal and understated, but it's just so cool and elegant. It's quite the opposite of what he becomes in the seventies and eighties. I couldn't really get with all that. To me that period from the late fifties up until the early seventies, I think that's Miles at his peak as a musician and also as a cultural figure and especially as a dresser.

What do you think his choice of clothing said about him as an artist and as a black man?

You put on your armor before you go out to do battle. When you're dealing with racism, when you're dealing with what it means to be a black man in America at the time Miles was doing his thing, you need every tool available to you to stand against that. So, the clothes you choose to wear and how you adorn yourself is more than just you're wearing your clothes because you have to, you're making a statement. You're making multiple statements: you're making a cultural statement; you're making an artistic statement and you're making a personal statement. I always say clothes is a person's sort of artistic statement to the world.

What Miles is saying is basically 'when you deal with me is a lot you have to deal with: I'm clean, I don't give a fuck. I talk shit, the place I live in is immaculate, I'm driving shit the average motherfucker can't afford'…he's basically saying 'you can't fuck with me. I'm not like the rest for you, I'm untouchable'. That always appealed to me. It was like 'get your shit together and put your armor on and go out in the street and do battle with this bullshit'. That's what I took from it: you gotta be clean. In the autobiography Miles is talking about what he got from observing Sugar Ray Robinson box. He said you have to have style in whatever you do, if it's boxing and if it's music, whatever you do, you gotta have style. He goes into this whole thing about the importance of style and how he brought that into his music. To me, style is active, not just something to look at, it's what you are. 'Clean', that's about respect. That's about dignity. That's about how you distinguish yourself from the masses.

It resonates, and that's why when you talk about Miles as an icon of style, he almost didn't have a peer, at least not in this period. God bless him, but Miles was a guy getting older and he was trying to fight with Father Time and Father Time of course is undefeated. So, you have Miles at a certain point following as opposed to leading. I think that's what you get in the seventies and eighties but that moment when he was leading, the spot between him and whoever was number two was huge.

Over the last few years his image has taken a few hits due to his reported treatment of women, some of which he himself acknowledged and expressed regret. How do you place that in the overall context of the man?

I remember when the autobiography came out and there were people at the time, women as well as white critics using Miles and his treatment of women as a way of criticizing his legacy. If you read the autobiography, the thing that is so great about it is the honesty. He's not denying it. That doesn't mean he should be praised for doing it, but Miles comes from a different generation and I think that sort of thing was tolerated a lot for that time, more so than the way people look at it now. You can see with the whole 'Me Too' thing a lot of this is generational because so many of these people that have been caught up are much older. That's not an excuse, it's just that like a lot of other things, it's not as though domestic violence or abuse was ever cool, but it was a lot more tolerated in previous times, or at least not discussed as much.

You have to look at Miles as you do any cultural figure for who they are. It's not just about hero worship, praising them as perfect individuals, because none of us are that. Miles had flaws. I think one flaw that's quite obvious is his treatment of women. I think if you look at most men of his generation who are that prominent, if you look at his background, you're going to find something similar. That's not an excuse, that's not a justification, but we're just now getting to a point where people are seriously dealing with domestic abuse, domestic violence, sexual assault. People are really just now starting to take that sort of thing seriously. Bill Cosby is a very old man of Miles' generation and he's in the penitentiary now because of that type of behavior.

If you look at that era you're going to find that that sort of thing was common and when you study any historical figures you have to be honest about the strengths and weaknesses of their character and you also have to recognize them for who they are at the time that they lived in and be careful not to hold them accountable for something that is the case now but wouldn't seem the same way then. To be clear, domestic violence, domestic abuse, sexual assault was never cool, but for men of the generation that Miles was a part of, it wasn't unusual for people to need to put hands on a woman to keep her 'in line'. He's a product of his time. Abraham Lincoln freed the slaves but if you actually go back and look at Abraham Lincoln's attitude about black people, it was overtly racist, but that doesn't mean they're going to stop talking about Abraham Lincoln. They're going to talk about him freeing the slaves. But they're probably not going to talk about his racism though, because his racism makes that other narrative a little harder to sell.

This is not to defend what happened, but that was just the way it was. I think the mistake is if you say, 'they did it back in the day and it wasn't a big deal' and now it is. It wasn't cool then and it's not cool now, but it was accepted in a way at that time that is no longer accepted. You look at it for what it is, and you learn from it. I think that's what we have to do is learn from it.

You can't say, 'why would you write a book about Miles when he beat his women?' I always tell people when they start that kind of shit, Martin Luther King slept with 3 different women the night before he got killed. He's a man, he's a human being. He's also this transcendent historical and cultural figure. I think the problem we have though is a lot of times people want to make these figures like they're gods. They're not. They're humans and humans have flaws and there's often a connection between those flaws and the art that they create. I've had similar conversations with people about Miles and I'm like I'm not going to stop talking about Miles, but I'm going to talk about Miles in a way that is informed and thorough. So, to me with Miles or whoever we're talking about, I think it's better if we look at these people in a more well-rounded way and so with that said, domestic violence is fair game, but you can't just erase him. This whole 'cancelled culture'? You can't cancel nobody. They existed! You can't just dismiss Miles because he doesn't fit with your contemporary version of how somebody should live their life. You have to find a way to recognize the good and the bad, that's what I think.

Final question: if there was another word besides 'cool' to describe Miles, what would it be?

I can't use 'cool'? I would say 'motherfucker', but I mean it in the best possible usage of that term. I don't know if a lot of people really understand the meaning of that word, but 'motherfucker' is like the word 'nigger': it can be positive, it can be negative, depending on the context. It can be the height of praise.

He was the ultimate motherfucker.

Jo Gelbard *was the last major relationship in Miles Davis' life. From 1984 until the end, Jo was his creative and life partner. Both married when they met, the relationship would be out in the open in 1985 following Miles' divorce from Cicely Tyson and Jo's divorce from her husband. Being an accomplished painter, Jo taught Miles how to paint, lighting a new creative fire that would last the rest of his life. Her memoir, 'Miles and Jo: A Love Story in Blue', chronicles the adventure that was their relationship.*

How did you and Miles meet?

In 1984. We met on an elevator. We lived in the same 5th Avenue building, 985 5th Avenue. He lived on the upper floor. He was married to Cicely (Tyson) and he was on crutches. He had just had hip replacement surgery and was just coming out of retirement.

What struck you first about him?

He was so intense. Like in the movie when the woman sees the vampire and she doesn't know if she's going to be killed or eaten or kissed and she doesn't care? That's how it was! He said, 'I wish I had your hair'. I said don't waste a wish. What if God is listening and all you get is my hair. Wish for more.' He just glared at me and I was nervous. I was going for a run in the park. Then he leaned over and said, 'you'd better run fast, 'cause I'll be back and I'm going to catch you'. I had no reply. I was just frozen. I was very inexperienced. I was a Jewish princess, married at eighteen. I had no experience in the world other than being married and being a mother.

I bet your run that day was a different kind of run.

It was a panicky run! If I could have run to the other side of the earth, I would have done that and kept going. But our relationship didn't take off for a long time. He was calling me over the intercom and would visit me at my apartment and I visited him at his. I mean, he was still on crutches, so there was no big affair going on. It was just very exciting for both of us.

When he said he wished he had your hair, was he already wearing

wigs then?

Oh, the hair issue! The hair issue was part of the clothes issue. There were huge hair issues all of the time. When I met him, he did not have all of those attachments and things, but it was an issue for him. Very important to him, always. And when he got sick, he was losing his hair. Then he moved into the braided things. The bald thing wasn't happening then. He missed that completely.

What do you think took him down the road of sartorial flamboyance that he embraced during his final decade?

The way he described it to me, he went from the suit and tie to an afro thing. That was his first change. When he could move around more freely, when he got rid of the suits and ties and was wearing African shirts, his music changed. So, every change in his life is linked to everything else, meaning his self-esteem, his self-image and therefore his music would change also. He was addicted to change. He decided he could be anything with his clothes.

So, the African thing changed his music. That was when he started walking around more. That's what he said to me. I don't track every decade of his life.

When I met him, everything was changing. He was coming out of retirement, he fell in love with me, and he started painting. He envisioned this whole new life with me. He left Cicely and moved into this new apartment, changed the entire décor to super modern. He collected art; he was painting. If you look at some of our art, you can see the changes throughout the seven years we were together, the optimism of the early paintings. They were very childlike and bright and happy and optimistic. That coincided with (Japanese designer) Koshin (Satoh) and they just went crazy with each other.

I felt like the clothes victimized him. He was a little guy. He was thin and not that healthy. So Koshin's clothes wore him.

Shoes were another thing that he was crazy about. It was nothing for him to buy a dozen pair at a time. These narrow, European shoes that hurt his feet. His feet were in terrible shape, because he had diabetes too, so his feet got worse. Then he found these Frankenstein shoes, which is what Koshin was doing. These heavy coats...everything was more creative, but it was stage clothing.

Then he got into the diaper pants, big baggy pants and print shirts. He loved those. That was his day look. He was always dressed at home. He used to say, 'I have to rehearse my clothing'. Even painting, he ruined all of his clothes when we were painting.

He'd wear his good clothes to paint?

Everything! And he'd spend a fortune on clothing. I couldn't even speak when I went shopping with him. He had very large print silk shirts that he wore with the tails out. He gave my son a speech, 'never ever tuck your shirt in'. When he got through the Koshin thing, I thought he'd look great in Versace because it wasn't as way out as Koshin, but wild prints. Which he looked beautiful in because his skin was so dark. At the end of our relationship, he was all in Versace.

We also painted a lot in colors. His environment, the apartment that I decorated was very colorful because it made him happy. I think the colors we were painting in the apartment led him into Versace.

He needed all of his clothes in front of him. At night mostly. It was like a nightmare. He wanted to look at them; everything. He said if he didn't see it, he wouldn't remember he had it. They were literally everywhere. He looked at his clothes all the time. He loved them. Maybe it was his fantasy of who he was going to be that day.

Back to the hair: did he go from extensions to full-on wigs?

No. Those were all extensions. He spent hours doing extensions. He was very dedicated to getting that right. It was so important to him that I thought 'maybe I should get him some extensions for the right look.' But he would have been great bald, he would have been beautiful. I suggested it, but he was not ready for it at all. The truth is that he was vulnerable and insecure at that point because he knew how sick he was. Had he been in top form, he would have gone bald. But he was feeling week, so he needed the extreme clothing and hair to prop him up.

Were you with him when he did the last Montreux show a few months before he died?

Yes. We both knew it was near the end of his life. I don't think he would have been touring much more. That last year of his life he pushed really hard to do too many things. He could have maybe lived longer if he had retired and took better care of himself, but he didn't and he wouldn't have liked that, so he wasn't going to die like that.

Montreux? He loved Gil (Evans). I think he loved Gil more than any other person. I think he was coming home. It was not painful for him to do. It was painful physically, but emotionally? It was touching and melancholy.

When did his health take that really bad turn? It seemed that he'd have bouts of sickness combined with bursts of good health intervals.

By 1985, everything was great. We were going to have this unbelievable life together. We had the art; we were having shows and everything was fantastic. Then he started to do too much. He had diabetes. He was a mess. He was always a mess. I don't know what he had before me, but I'm sure he had heart events or mini strokes from all of the abuse that he had done.

He came into our relationship in pretty bad shape. Then he pulled up, but then he started to believe his own stories that he was Superman. He'd work too much: he'd film, then he'd go on tour, then he was recording. He was eating sugar; he was too weak. He was very self-destructive with his lifestyle. When you're diabetic, you have to take your health much more seriously than he did.

What would you say was the most challenging part of the relationship?

That's a long list. He was extremely possessive, jealous and needy. There were not enough moments in the day that I could be dedicated to him. Nothing I did or said or executed was ever enough. He wanted everything. I was already the subservient wife. He had the perfect woman in me. I was rich, I didn't need him for his shit, but I needed him for what he was saying to me. I didn't need the glamour or the clothing or the money. It was the perfect storm, except that I grew. But it didn't matter because he died. I often wonder how long I could have stayed with him because I was changing. He changed me so much. Certainly, if I met him now, I couldn't be with him.

Did you see any changes in him as time progressed?

He was so loving and needy and poetic. I don't know what he was like earlier in his life, but he was so romantic when he wasn't demanding and jealous and paranoid. But I was having an affair with him, so a lot of that pressure should have been there. I wasn't his until the last year. I don't have affairs with married people anymore (laughs).

The last year I was divorced, so we could be out in the open together and he took me to Bloomingdales. It was like a Cinderella movie. I'd always buy his clothes. I bought most of his clothes, ten-twenty thousand in a shot with him. He'd always say, 'buy something', but I never cared about clothes. But when I left my husband, I needed to be next to 'Miles Davis', I needed to look ok. So, he took me to Bloomingdales and got me dressed in a private room and he kept bringing in clothes. I felt like Audrey Hepburn, going to the ball.

Did he have a good eye for you?

He was an excessive shopper. He'd buy twenty suits in a shot. He didn't give it a lot of thought. That addictive personality translated itself into shopping as well. When he dressed me, it was conservative. I don't think he wanted anyone looking at me.

How did the painting come into play?

He asked me to teach him how to paint, so I got him the supplies. But I didn't want to over teach him. Then he got all involved with the paint like a kid, just fun. Then one day he said, 'we've got to change'. Then it was more intention. It was a big challenge and we were getting places. He saw the development and it excited him. His art progressed very rapidly.

He's been gone for over twenty years now. What's it like for you these days when you think of him?

To this day, there are compliments about his music and his fashion and things, but as a person, they make him out to be not so great. Maybe his wives or lovers talked to you in a loving way, but the public opinion I find is about the Prince of Darkness who slept with hookers and beat up women. My intention was to show his loving side in my book. That's why I wrote it.

If you could describe him in a single word, what would it be?
'Passion'.

Koshin Satoh *is an experimental designer whose futuristic fashion and textiles captured the imagination of Miles Davis, who wore his clothes through the last decade of his life. From his home in Japan, Sato-san kindly consented to an email interview about his impressions and memories of Miles Davis:*

How did you and Miles meet? When he came to Tokyo, a person from Yomiuri newspaper brought him to my office.

Were you a fan of his music prior to the meeting at your office?

I wasn't a fan before meeting him.

What was the initial meeting like?

I was shocked as I met the alien.

What was inspiring about him?

His thinking was always positive.

How did you create for him?

After receiving an offer to custom design for the Grammy Awards, I sent the design drawings via fax. I started making clothes after getting his OK.

What was it like to create clothing for Miles?

He didn't hear a thing I said. For example, I made a top and bottom set, but he wore them separately.

How would you describe his fashion sense, his style?

He asked for the new, always. And he changed them to his own style.

What was most surprising about him?

That he wore any type of dress very well. He looks good in anything, even if it was too big for him.

Was there a favorite garment that you created for him, or that he was particularly fond of?

I don't mean to be cocky, but he liked all of the clothes that I made.

Any memorable stories about him as it relates to fashion?

When he did a fashion show in New York, he didn't come to rehearsal and came in 10 minutes before the start of the show. He said, 'there is no need for rehearsal, to me'.

I had the location of shooting a catalog in New York in February. When I finished about half the shooting, he said, 'try to shoot the rest at my house tomorrow, because I will die from the cold'. And the shooting was called off.

Now, more than 20 years since his death, what comes to mind when you think of Miles Davis?

He's still alive in my head. He often talks to me.

If you could describe Miles Davis in a single word, what would it be?

親友 ('Best Friend' in Japanese)

*One of the most accomplished and versatile musicians on the planet, **Marcus Miller** was also one of the most important people in Miles Davis' final decade. Having served on different occasions as bassist, producer and cheerleader on several of Miles' final albums, Miller was a trusted confidante, sounding board and creative inspiration for Davis. Miller's understanding of contemporary music, as evidenced by his success co-writing and co-producing for the likes of Luther Vandross and others, helped Miles navigate a shift to a more accessible sound while still forging new ground. When I reached out to him, he was very happy to talk with me about one of the most influential people in his life and career.*

What was your professional relationship with Miles?

I was the bass player in his band when he came out of retirement from his Seventies seclusion in 1981.

Did you meet him as an active musician before he came out of retirement?

I had never met Miles. I had gotten a call about a year earlier, from a contractor named Gene Bianco. He said Miles was coming out of retirement and is putting together a band for this session. I showed up at the session, Miles never showed up. When I actually got the call from Miles, like a year later, the first thing I said was 'are you gonna be there?' He said, 'yeah motherfucker, if you gonna be there'. I said, 'that sounds like Miles to me!'

What was that like for you when you met him?

Man, it was incredible. Because he had been in retirement for so long, I wasn't really clear if he really existed, except for the rumors! He showed up at that studio a couple of hours after he called me, and to see the guy walk in the door as a real human being was a trip?

How did he look?

He was about five feet shorter than I thought he'd be, 'cause I thought he was at least eight feet tall. He was 5'6" or 7, not a big guy at all. But his voice was exactly like everybody had been imitating, he was as different a cat as you'd expect him to be. A lotta cats when you meet them, you're kind of disappointed that they're actually human beings. You see 'em drinking water, you see 'em hailing cabs, you see 'em doing stuff that regular people do. But with Miles, he was really a unique cat.

What stood out the most to you when you met him?

The way he expressed himself was very cryptic and full of imagery. He would say stuff like 'make sure it's on the up, not the down, and then circle it sometimes'. I immediately understood everything he said. The way he was telling me actually gave me more instruction than if he had said it in a way that everyone understood. He was saying 'I don't want to tell you exactly what to do, because then there's no room for you to contribute', and that's what everyone who plays with Miles gets to do, is to contribute, on a large scale.

Sometimes he'd give me instructions that were non-verbal. He'd give me a key, and then I'd play a bassline, he'd shake his head 'no'. I'd play another one, he'd shake his head 'no'. I'd play a third one, he'd nod his head 'yes'. That was it, that was all the instruction I got. I quickly learned not to ask him so much.

With the more cryptic style of communication, it opened things up for me. It made me ask more questions about myself. It makes you dig into yourself. And, because it's Miles, you care. You really want to give him something good. So, you dig down. It makes you a better musician.

What happened next?

After the two years I played in his band, I left to develop more as a producer and composer. When I came back to him, he left Columbia and came to Warner Bros. I called Warner Bros. and they said Miles was looking to do something different and asked if I had any material. I sent over some stuff I had been working on and started writing stuff.

I flew out to California to present the stuff. We recorded without Miles there. Miles came in to listen and gave me his blessing. He'd say, 'write another section. It needs another section' and then leave. But because it's

Miles, you put whatever is inside of you into the request. I've gotta write a nice section, I've gotta write something that hasn't been done before, because this is Miles.

Had he changed in the two years since you'd seen him?
There was a huge difference because when I was in the band the first time, he was still doing blow, and he was in really bad health. He was the closest I'd ever seen anybody to the end. We did a gig at Saturday Night Live and he was just pacing. We had just come from Japan. I asked him, 'why you keep walking? You won't stop walking'. He said, 'I'm afraid if I stop walking, I won't be able to start again'. That's how bad he was doing.

But towards the end of my stay with Miles, he got married to Cicely (Tyson), and she got him onto acupuncture, holistic treatments and got him to stop whatever he was doing. When I came back two years later, he was a different cat. He was erratic when I was first with him and his sound wasn't strong. When I came back, he was alert, his eyes were clear, and those first few hours I kept saying, 'Man, you look so good'. He said, 'alright motherfucker, I got it! I look good. Shut up!' But that was when I got to benefit from being in his presence, because he was clear.

What made your musical relationship with him special?

I was very much a contemporary musician: I play jazz, I play funk, r&b, but I was very knowledgeable about the history of jazz and Miles' whole history, I knew his whole story. I think other contemporary guys who were trying to write for Miles might not have been familiar with his whole story. When you listen to whatever I did with Miles, it sounds like the contemporary music of the time, there were references to the rest of his life and I think that made him comfortable and it gave him a focus. You've got to have something in mind for him. You've gotta have a melody, a direction.

I had everything laid out for *Tutu*. I knew what I wanted him to play, but I was a little intimidated at first, because he was Miles Davis. The Tutu track is playing, and he can see that I've got this energy, and he says, 'when are you going to tell me what to do? I know you know what you want me to do, so stop bullshitting, let's hear it'. I said, 'I need you to play this melody here and blah blah blah'. And once you gave him that, then he could become Miles Davis.

The melodies I knew, I knew what Miles' range was, what sounds good for him. I knew what sounded good for him that day, because his chops weren't strong yet. I was writing for him with a full knowledge of what he was all about.

What type of clothes was he wearing in those days?
When I first met him, he was wearing some weird stuff: headbands, you could tell he was in transition. After the first *Man with the Horn* session, he said 'come by my house tomorrow'. I showed up the next day, he's listening to what we had recorded the day before. He was pretty crazy then. He said, 'help me find something to wear for the session today'.

So, I went into the bedroom and I opened the closet and all of the clothes were from ten years ago! Bellbottoms and fringes, all these crazy colors and the shoes had these little platforms and heels on them. I was like 'Miles, there's nothing in here that we can work with. You can't be wearing nothing from here'. He started putting on layers of stuff. Like, it would look like 1975 if you put one outfit on, but if you put layers of 2-3 at the same time, it looked like some futuristic stuff. That's how he got by that day. He had on three jackets!

When we went on the road, the stuff he was wearing wasn't that remarkable, style-wise. You could tell he was just starting to get himself back together. He was trying to figure out if he was going to go with the mustache; he had a trucker's hat one time. He was trying to find his chops on the trumpet, and he was trying to find his style chops too.

By the time I came back in 1985, he had settled into this Japanese, Koshin Satoh kind of style. Shoulder pads, really bright shiny colors, the fabrics were really interesting, the shoes were crazy. That's the style that carried him through the end of his life. Koshin Sato was a very contemporary designer and Miles was into it.

Eventually I'd be at his house in New York to work on some music. We'd do that and then he'd say, 'ok, we've gotta try on some clothes'. Since I was the one closest in size to Miles, he'd make me put the clothes on, then have me stand in front of him and his buddies while he decided if he liked it or not. He'd look at something and say, 'naw, I don't like that. You keep that'. Whatever he didn't like, I had got to put in my bag! It was expensive stuff, very cutting-edge stuff. But he was so into it.

Why do you think that was?

He came from an era where blacks were just coming out of that obligatory, minstrel-y, smiley and being very Stepin Fetchit about their presentation. It was the only way you could be a performer. Miles detested that, to be entertainers instead of artists. So, when the bebop movement came, it was a true movement. We're artists, we have our own language, we have our own lifestyle, which is not so much about smiling or being entertainers. I mean, if that's who you are, that's cool.

When Miles first came from St. Louis to New York, he wanted to join this language, this world, this culture. He was already style-conscious, but Dexter Gordon said 'you can't hang out with us with that Brooks Brothers shit. If you're going to hang with us, you got to go up to J&J's in Harlem and get fitted out.'

The clothes were as much of the culture as anything else. I think he never let that go. He was really one of those cats who would consider what he wore before he stepped out of the house. When was I being initialized during the seventies, it was all about fusion, and those guys looked like they didn't pay attention to what they wore at all. That was the evolution. The first evolution was 'we need to command respect as musicians. We're going to be so impeccably dressed that no one's going to question our sophistication and the fact that we need to be respected. That's the first step.

The next step in the mid-sixties was, 'we've come so far, we don't need to prove anything to you anymore. Now, you're not even worthy of being impressed. We're gonna wear what we want'. In the seventies, cats were wearing their 'fros all crazy. When I came up, there wasn't as much emphasis on that.

It was interesting to meet Miles, who was bringing that aesthetic: 'It's really important the way you present yourself'. At the same time, I was I joining Miles' band, Wynton Marsalis, young cats, my age were dressing like Miles dressed in the fifties, going 'this is what jazz is'. It came back.

How would you say you discovered your own unique style?

Wearing the clothes Miles gave me and realizing it doesn't work. You can't put on somebody else's clothes, you can't talk like somebody else, and you can't play like somebody else. If you're going to be a real artist, you have to find your own thing. For me, it was a gradual process; I had to find stuff that looked good on me, not stuff that looks good hanging, or stuff that looks good on somebody else. It's hard to do man, because clothes are an extension of your life. The same way that you have to get comfortable with the way you look, you have to get comfortable with the way you sound as a musician and embrace it. I mean, it's so much easier to play like somebody else, because they did all of the hard work! If you play like Thelonious Monk, nobody's gonna boo you, they booed Monk when he first started playing like that, because nobody's heard it before. He did all the hard work; you're just following in his path. But what about finding your own path, taking the lumps that come along with that? Clothes are the same thing. It's all about style, man. That's what Americans value the most and that's what the world values about American culture, is style. It takes a minute, but it's really about self-acceptance.

What did you think of Miles' style?

Like everybody, the style in the fifties and sixties was classic and timeless. You could tell he spent so much time, not only on his clothes but his hair. He had the right clothes for the right situation. You can see in the recording studio he wasn't wearing a suit. He'd have on a cool shirt, maybe a scarf. This cat put a lot of time into considering what was appropriate.

Clothing style is like music. Miles is somebody who was fiercely dedicated to 'now'. When he came to New York in the forties, it was because he was amazed at the music that Charlie Parker and Dizzy were playing, because it was music of that particular time. It was cool, it was deep, it incorporated the dance rhythms of that time, so everything about it was modern.

People say he kept changing, but he really didn't. He was always going after the same thing. As soon as the music represented an older era, he moved on to what was hip, what was deep, what was reflective of the now. Style wise, he was pretty much the same thing. His clothes represented the fifties, the sixties, the seventies he had another style. In the eighties, I said to him, 'what do you think about these young cats who are just coming on the scene, dressed like you in the sixties? What do you think about them playing in the style that you were playing in the sixties?' He said, 'you know what I see when I hear that music? Bell-bottom pants'. For him, the music is so inextricably tied to the times, that when he hears that sound, he see the clothes, he sees the dance, he sees the hair that people wore. It was as crazy to ask him to play the music from fifteen years ago as to ask him to wear the clothes from fifteen years ago.

To that point, why do you think he did the Montreux concert with Quincy Jones in 1991, revisiting the old music that he swore he'd never play again?

It was the first time he did it, and he was gone, what, four months later? As far as I'm concerned, I don't which happened because of which. I don't know if he did the show because on some level, he knew that he didn't have a lot of time left, or when he finally did address his past, that that kind of triggered something in him.

On one level, I'm really glad he did that Montreux thing. I always wanted Miles to stop at some point and look behind him, to see what he created. There are five generations of musicians whose lives he changed. He changed music! I don't know if he really understood what was going on behind him. For him it was really important that at some point, he'd turn around and go 'oh shit, really?' I think Montreux had a little bit to do with that. But as soon as he decided to look back, I think the Montreux was in the summer and he passed away in September.

He was starting to let go of a lot of stuff. He was beginning to smile at the audience, a lot of stuff that you'd never see him do. I think in a certain respect, he was wrapping things up.

Talk to me about Miles modeling his clothes.

(Laughs) Before he decided to make me wear the clothes. He'd put on something, get in front of the mirror and (feigns drawing two pistols) and shoot at himself in the mirror. That was the coolest thing you could do. It was a pretty old-fashioned move, but you could just tell, being cool was important to him. It was part of that culture.

There was an era in black music where the whole thing was to make it look effortless. It was all about making it look easy. It was about everything having no rough edges. That style that Miles had in the fifties was about the same thing. There were no rough edges, everything was right.

There's a really popular black and white video of Miles with Trane, Paul Chambers, Wynton Kelly on the piano and Jimmy Cobb on the drums. I played it for Miles, and he said, 'man, you can't tell, but that's a green gabardine suit. He said it was cold-blooded, but the big thing was that I didn't have a tie on'. He wore a scarf and that was a big deal. At that time, late fifties, early sixties, a tie was a part of your presentation. These things are so tied together.

Miles was a complete artist, man. The trumpet was his most potent tool, but it was all about self-expression. If you look at his artwork, you can tell a lot about him through his art. You could tell stuff about him through his music that you couldn't tell from talking with him! He had a gruff exterior to a lot of people, a lot of layers of protection that he had. But when you heard him play *My Funny Valentine*, you knew there was a sensitive soul, you can't play that without it. You couldn't always believe what Miles said, but you could always believe what he played.

What's the Savoy story?

We were playing there; it was an electric band and kind of loud. He's facing me, but the combination of his raspy voice and the volume of the band, I couldn't understand what he was saying. I'm like, am I doing something wrong, because he's really trying to get me to hear what he's saying. The band finally came down and he said, 'how you like these shoes?' I said, 'man those are some nice shoes! Where'd you get them?' He said, 'Cicely got them for me. What size you wear. I'll have her get you a pair'. This is while the band is playing! The audience is looking at us thinking, man Miles must be dropping some cold-blooded musical information on Marcus!

Is there something about Miles that people would be surprised to know?

His humanity. He was really interested in people that he was interested in. He'd watch you. The way you walk, the way you talked. If he gave you a gift, a piece of clothing, it would fit you perfectly. He was so into regular human stuff. He was so perceptive.

What was the best thing about working with Miles?

It was amazing to write something and know that you had the most expressive voice in the history of jazz to play that stuff. The other thing is because it was Miles, it made me find something that I probably wouldn't have found if I was writing for someone else.

The most important thing was how fiercely dedicated he was to being himself. He embraced himself. He was not apologetic. It sounds easy, it sounds like a cliché, but when you really get into it, and you realize how many times you deny yourself, you go, 'I shouldn't be like this, I wish I was like that'. And he had to go through that himself. At some point in his life, end of the forties, early fifties, all of a sudden, he discovered all of the things that we love Miles for.

Hanging around him, you see how committed you have to be, to be yourself. And I'm still learning, I'm still kind of getting it together, but that was the biggest lesson. Thelonious Monk said, 'a genius is somebody who's the most like himself'. 'Figure out who you are and be the hell out of that'. I think that's the message I got from Miles.

If you could describe him in a single word, what would it be?

'Himself'. 100%, himself. He got so much criticism throughout his life. Despite what you might think about him, he was a very sensitive individual. Whatever people said, I'm sure some of those things got inside and probably hurt him. But it never changed his direction or his idea about what he should be doing. You gotta take your hits, but you've gotta stay on your path.

Mikel Elam is a successful painter, whose work has been featured internationally, and he received a bachelor's degree in Studio Arts/ Painting from the University of the Arts in Philadelphia. During his creative journey, Mikel spent time as Miles Davis' assistant.

How did you and Miles hook up?

In 1987 I was a couple of years out of art school, unemployed and had a friend who had started getting into jazz. The band saw her, she was very beautiful, and they invited her backstage. Miles sees her and kind of takes her under his wing. They became friends for a short period of time, but it didn't last that long.

At one point, he tells her he's looking for an assistant and she gave my name. She thought I had the right disposition for him. I met him on a Thursday, and I was on a plane for Europe the next day.

It sounds like a short interview?

It was a long interview with the management people. I got there at 11 o'clock and interviewed with Peter Schukat and Gordon Meltzer. They called over to Miles at the Essex House to see if he wanted to interview me. He said no, he'd be ready at 5. They sent me out with money to get lunch and go over to the embassy to get a visa. I did it, but I didn't know travel was for the next day!

I get back over to the office at 430. I meet Miles and he hands me a sketchbook that he's been drawing in and asks me, 'what do you think of this?' I look into it and say 'oh, it's nice', I mean, what else am I going to say? He's sitting there and I'm shaking in my boots. You want to talk about style? He's dressed to the nines. He had on a gray jacket with sparkles going through it. It was fabulous, cut like a blazer, kind of like an anthracite; very metallic looking and I think he had on black leather pants. He told me he liked the jacket I was wearing. One of my friends, Patrick Bushnell, became a designer for him for a few years. He loaned me a jacket to wear, and Miles asked me where I got it. I told him and he didn't say anything, he just took note.

When I went on the road with him, I had a few clothes from Patrick and every time I wore something, he'd say, 'where'd you get that?' and that's how the whole dialogue started to get Pat to make him clothes.

The whole intensity of him, shopping and everywhere we went was out of control. The last words he said to me before I was hired was 'you're gonna love Europe. We're going to do a lot of shopping there'. Gordon said, 'you've got get home, get packed, we're leaving for Europe at 6 o'clock tomorrow'.

What was it like spending that kind of time with him?

The crew and the band called me 'Iron Mike'. When we were on the road, my days were sixteen to eighteen-hour days. Miles didn't sleep very much; he was excited about everything. He had the television going, the music going, magazines. He had a telephone. He had to have constant influx of communication. And this is pre-cell phone days and pre-computers. I'm convinced he'd be on top of all of it now if he was alive.

I made myself available to him, which meant I'd fall asleep in a chair, but that was cool. If it was 3 o'clock and he wake me up and say, 'hey can you go get me some watermelon?' All kinds of ridiculous requests.

At a certain point there were places that he was reclusive and places that he wanted to go out. It got to the point where he would send me shopping for him if he didn't feel like going. He started to trust my sensibility. Between 1987-1991, 30% of it (his wardrobe) that I probably purchased for him, without him ever seeing it. At a certain point I did get good at it. In the beginning he threw me into some of that, right away. On the first tour, we started in Belgium and ended up in France, and he said 'go out and buy me some stuff. I trust you'.

I was cautious. I bought stuff on sale. I was thinking from my vantage point. He never wore the first things that I bought. He put them in his trunk. By year number two, I got really in tuned to what he was wearing, so I'd go to Gautier, Versace, wherever we were if he didn't feel like going. Sometimes he would send me first and that would cause him to want to go back and get more the next time around. It was an endless pool of shopping wherever we went. If there's a store, let's go shopping.

Can you talk about his style during this period of working with him?

Yeah. He was out there. When I started, there were a lot of jackets that weren't really tailored, but with great differences. They were cut like a man's suit jacket, but they might have oversized shoulders in fabrics I'd never seen before for a man's jacket. He had leather pants in every color. He had lizard shoes and boots. He had big leather and shearling coats. Fashion was getting very avant-garde. He had a fashion show with Andy Warhol, where he was asked to model, at the Tunnel. That when he met Koshin Sato. Koshin's work was very avant-garde and Miles wore anything he sent him. In Japan, it was slightly retro but slightly futuristic at the same time. Koshin had a style that was like the early dandys of the 1900s except they were in this futuristic kind of color and fabric. A lot of them were shiny, and glitter, rubber, materials like that.

When we got to Japan, he went to Koshin and he must've spent $50,000 in ten minutes. It was everything he showed him. Miles never said 'no' to anything, whether he said it or not. He said, 'sometimes you gotta buy stuff and sit on it 'til it hits you'. Another line was 'you gotta rehearse outfits before you wear it'. I can't tell you how many times he'd be posing all day.

Are there any particular outfits that stood out for you?

One that he gave me. It was an Issey Miyake blow up rubber jacket. When I first saw him in it, I couldn't believe it and he actually ended up giving it to me. I just saved it because I'd never seen anything like it. I think I wore it one time to a special event. It was like a scuba diver, but it was black rubber. It was the first tour that we were on, this kind of flying around high style was new to me. We got off the plane and the press was around, and he got off the plane in that jacket and I'm looking at the silhouette thinking 'that is outrageous. Whose dream am I in?'

His glasses changed too. He went from the goggles to Porsche style glasses. He always had some kind of funky glasses on and he always had a lot of them. On each tour he probably had 5-6 pair of glasses.

Were there any pieces that he tended to favor?

There were clothes that he favored in 1987 that he wouldn't favor in 1988 or '89. Nothing anything too distinguishing that was overlapping, nothing that would basically transcend. Like that rubber jacket, he loved it, but he probably only wore it once or twice at best.

Do you remember the last time you saw him?

I found out he was in the hospital at St. Johns, he said to come on over and bring some fried chicken. His fascination with food! He knew what was in my neighborhood. He said there's a fried chicken place around the corner from you that's really good.

So, I brought him the chicken, he was sitting in a chair and he seemed fine, but something seemed different. After our visit I said I'll come back tomorrow and he said 'fine, just call before you come'. I remember that was different because he never said, 'call me before you come'. He used to say 'don't call; maybe you'll wake me up. Just come on over'. Then I called the next day and didn't get any answer. He went into a coma. We spent almost a month going to the hospital and then it ended.

What was that like for you?

I was crushed. I really thought he'd pull out of it. But the doctors said that there was going to be paralysis. In the long run, he wouldn't have been happy. Part of his whole thing was he was very much into doing what he wanted to do. I think he would have been miserable. I really cared about him and thought he was too young to die. I missed him for a long time and I still do. In my head, there are moments when I hear his music and he's there.

I don't have a ton of photos, but I have some. I wanted him to feel that he didn't always have to sign something or pose for a photograph. But the memories are in my head.

What do you think would most surprise people about him?

I don't think people understand how hysterically funny he could be. And he did it in a deadpan way which made it even funnier to me.

Do you consider any of his albums a favorite?

I like them all for different reasons, but there are different things in **Bitches Brew** that I'm drawn back to that CD, but on the other hand, I can play **Kind of Blue** over and over and it doesn't bother me.

If you could describe Miles Davis in one word, what would it be?

'Electric'.

Vince Wilburn Jr. is an accomplished drummer and producer who also oversees the Miles Davis estate with  *his cousins Cheryl Ann Davis, Erin Davis alongside the estate manager Darryl Porter. The estate has successfully introduced the artistry of Miles via deluxe music collections, a book of his artwork, the outstanding documentary Birth of the Cool and a US postage stamp with more to come. Vince has been at the forefront of it, making sure 'The Chief's' legacy continues to grow. Vince was instrumental in helping me get access to a number of the interviews you've enjoyed on the previous pages, and it felt only right for him to have the last word.*

When you think of Miles now, what comes to mind?

I'm thinking about musically, how many lives his music continues to touch and the global impact it has, on how different musicians seem to hold him in high reverence, you know?

For example, Daryl (Jones) is playing with the Rolling Stones and I've talked to (Stones drummer) Charlie Watts about Miles. I just read this book by Marvin Gaye's wife (*After the Dance: My Life with Marvin Gaye by Jan Gaye*), and she mentioned that Miles and Marvin were supposed to get together, but Miles didn't want to come to LA and Marvin didn't want to go to New York to record.

Tell me about the relationship with 'Uncle Miles'. Is that what you called him?

I bounced from 'Uncle Miles' to 'Chief'. As a young kid, I knew that he had impact, because of how my mom would always get my hair cut, dress me up and go down and he'd let me check the band from the side of the stage. I always looked forward to him coming to Chicago. And that was the time back in the day when you could meet the plane at the gate. It was cool to walk to the gate and then walk back with him and everybody knew him, like the skycaps. And a lot of people in airports. So that was kind of cool.

How was he when people approached him?

Just super cool, just waving. Everybody gave him his space. He was cool. He was always cool to see musicians that came backstage, cats that played with him back in the day. But he was pretty cool with people. People said that he was arrogant and unapproachable. I'm sure it was there, but I never experienced it that way in terms of him greeting the public.

So how did your relationship with him evolve over time from you as a kid to you as a young man to you as a player in your own right?

Well, my mom told him I wanted to play drums. He said, 'well, get him a cheap kit and if he sticks to it, then we'll get him a professional kit'. So that's what happened. I think we got it from Monroe or Sears. It was a blue sparkle kit and I was so serious about it. I just beat the heck out of it. I played it every day, every day.

Was he keeping an eye on you?

Yeah, he'd call and talk to my mom about 'how's Vince coming with his groups"'

Around '79 or '80, he had taken some time off and was thinking about coming back. He would call and have my mom take the phone off the hook so he can listen to us. Then he would critique us and say, 'you're getting there, you guys want to make a record?' And next thing you know, Dr. George Butler (head of Columbia Records Jazz division) flew us to New York. They picked us up in a stretch limo and then we went to 30th street to do *Man with the Horn*.

I saw him when he toured that album and he came out in a loose pink jumpsuit and clogs with a knit cap. He was taking his time, moving slowly. He looked like he was dressed to be comfortable and relaxed. Was that kind of where it was at back then?

Yeah, I think those jumpsuits were from Issey Miyake and he had different colors. He was getting stronger and stronger with *Man with the Horn*. Then they recorded *We Want Miles*. The more he played, the stronger he got. It's like he got the motor running again.

What would you say was the most valuable lesson or advice that he gave or taught you?

You gotta be serious man. You can't fuck around and you gotta, you gotta study it. Don't be afraid to take chances and explore but take the music seriously. Don't bullshit the music or you're not a musician. I watched him listen to board tapes, studio tapes and always evolving and improving. He was reaching for something to make the music move forward until the day he couldn't play the music anymore.

That amazed me because it wasn't about the money. He had the money and house and fame, but it was the passion and love for the music. That's what I try to adhere to.

What do you think people didn't know about him that would surprise them if they did?

That he cared. He wasn't the fucking prince of darkness. He cared about his family. If he dug you, he cared. He cared about you.

He was an intelligent, astute businessman. He was well-versed and he was a hell of a chef. He had this little phone book filled with menus and we can't find that damned book to this day. He made bouillabaisse, he made his own sauce, but he would never eat anything. But that's probably why he stayed so small because he liked cooking for other people. He told me about the time he made of a couple of ducks and Buddy Miles sat and at both of them! There was a deli on Broadway and 77th and I used to run out and get fresh vegetables for him.

If I say Miles and clothes, what's the first thing that comes to mind?

I've never seen anybody change clothes five to six times a day. He called it 'rehearsing'. He would lay them out in the morning, then after a couple of hours, he'd look up and he had something else on. Look up again, and he'd have something else on. If we went swimming at Pepperdine, he came back with something else. I guess that's the way his mind was working.

He told me when I used to go shopping, never look at the price tag. That was because he just picked what he wanted. These stores would just let him pick whatever he wanted, and they'd bill the accountant. In his mind, when he saw something he liked, he would know how it would 'drape' on him as he called it, and they would pack it up and send it to the house. I mean five, ten, fifteen, twenty thousand dollars, it didn't matter.

Did he ever wear jeans?

I never saw him in jeans, but he had some denim overalls that he used to paint in, but for the most part, I don't remember any denim. I do remember some denim onstage.

Marcus Miller told me that Miles used to paint in his regular clothes too.

He did! We had this big glass dining room table in Malibu, and we had a hell of a time getting the paint off this big, long assed table. But he wasn't into cleaning up.

We had housekeepers and people to clean up, but his mind didn't think like that. I remember when he would paint, if he wasn't finished with it, sometimes he would take it off, hang it up and look at it right on the wall, taped on the wall, take it back off the wall and continue to work on it until he thought it was finished.

In the later years when he started wearing the genie pants and those huge shoulder pads with the really big hair, did he ever talk to you about his style?

I know he and Nick Ashford of Ashford and Simpson essentially had the same cat, I think his name was Kevin, and he used to make these big shirts with the shoulder pads, and some had studs in them. He never really talked about it; he just didn't want anybody on the bandstand to look out of place.

I remember I had a bunch of Nike stuff on one day, and he told me, 'you look like a fucking walking billboard'. When he said that I had to take the Nike stuff off and get into some hip clothes. I mean it was with love. It wasn't like he was trying to bust my ass, but he was! You gotta play your ass off and look good playing your ass off.

At least look hip. We couldn't afford the shit he was wearing; you know what I mean. Koshin Satoh and all those cats, we couldn't afford that. We had to make do with what our salaries could afford. I think Issey did give us some jumpsuits. We'd go to dinner with him when we went to Japan…nice gentleman.

Did he ever give you fashion advice or suggestions?

Just think about what you wear when you're out because the clothes are an extension of you.

One day he told me, when you eat your soup, take the spoon away from the bowl. He was into shit like that. You can never be shocked by the things you could learn from him. Be it cars, cooking, clothes and on top of that, the music was like foremost the main shit.

He used to always send us out to get him European fashion magazines, the big thick ones.

What do you think it was about the Japanese designers that Miles was so attracted to?

I guess the fact that they would make things to fit his body. Those designers loved him so much that they just made the things that he liked. They'd send him designs and he just dug it.

I remember a guy, Franco Pachetti, that made his shoes up on Fairfax Blvd. And I remember a guy named Mario had made his Italian suits, and then the twins in Europe, Lancy and Laria, who he called 'Same Thing'. They were making some of his clothes.

Was there any particular outfit or piece of clothing that stood out for you?

It was all cool. I remember when we were in Japan, he used to wear these tank tops designed by Koshin. We were doing a series of outdoor Japanese concerts. By that time, we were all wearing Koshin's pieces.

Aside from the music, what is the most valuable thing you got from Miles, either directly or inspirationally?

Aside from the music, just be true to yourself. Don't bullshit people, don't bullshit yourself.

He had a sense of humor, he liked to laugh, but it was about taking care of business and that's the main thing I got from him: take care of your business, kick-ass on your instrument and move the music forward.

How would you describe him in a single word?

'Explorer', because he always looked to the future.

Every time we would rehearse, or he would critique us after each concert, he would tell us to try something different. And it always worked. He had an uncanny way of knowing that it would.

.

ABOUT THE AUTHOR

Michael Stradford is a multi-decade entertainment executive. He has successfully programmed radio stations in several major markets, including Los Angeles. Stradford was a senior executive in the music industry and enjoyed a long run as a creator of content for Sony Pictures Home Entertainment and oversaw original content at Sony owned online outlet, Crackle.com. Upcoming books include a pseudo memoir disguised as a book of movie reviews, 'Black to the Movies' and a coffee table book on Steve Holland, the world's greatest male model. He has written reviews, profiles and interviews for several magazines as well as running his own pop culture blog, lookingforthecool.com, with a podcast of the same name coming in development. Stradford lives in wedded bliss in Southern California with his tolerant wife Sybil and two equally tolerant dogs, Raj and Teddy.

Printed in Great Britain
by Amazon